	DUE DATE	08 Buc
ReTurn	Borrower	

THE NEW LAITY

Between Church and World

Ralph D. Bucy

WORD BOOKS
PUBLISHER
4800 WEST WACO DRIVE
WACO, TEXAS
76703

To
HOWARD AND PEGGY BLAKE
our mutual pastors,
without whom the Dallas conference or
this book would never have become a reality.

Acknowledgments

First of all the editor is deeply grateful to the writers themselves for the excellent quality of the essays. Without the genuine cooperation and considerable talent represented here, this book would have never been born.

In large measure, the encouragement to conceive of this book and to see it through to a successful conclusion came from Howard and Peggy Blake. The conference "The Laity—A New Direction," held at the University of Dallas, June, 1976, was their idea originally, and the personal invitation of Howard in our home in Galveston started my involvement and the exciting challenge of the subsequent development of this book. This is basically why this book is dedicated to them in recognition of their impact on my life and ministry.

The idea of a book developed while Mike Murray and I were working on the In-depth report of the conference. The momentum was sustained at the meeting of the planning committee in Cincinnati in December 1976, especially the encouragement of Howard Blake, Dick Mouw, Joe Gremillion, Jim Rice, and Mike Murray.

James I. McCord, the President of Princeton Theological Seminary, played a major role in the conference and in supporting the preparation of this book. He was particularly helpful to me personally, as we discussed the concept, contributors, and content on two separate occasions. To continue our close personal friendship which began years ago when he was Dean of Austin Seminary and I was one of his students is one of the blessings coming out of the process of preparation. All of us regret profoundly that he could not provide one of the essays. Several others were invited to write essays, but for good reasons could not. The warm and gracious letter from Dr. Theodore Hesburgh, President of the University of Notre Dame, is among the tokens of encouragement I have received.

My special thanks go to Word, Inc., especially to Jarrell McCracken and to Floyd Thatcher, who have gently guided me through the process of getting this book into print.

To my wife, June, to our sons, Pat, Flynn, and Tom, and to our daughters by marriage, Pam and Carolyn, I owe more than words can possibly express.

Contents

The Flavor of New Directions

Ralph D. Bucy*

Introduction

THIS BOOK IS AN EXPANSION OF A GROUP
of exciting ideas concerning the laity at work in the world.
The churches have enlisted laypersons through the years
to work and serve within the corporate structures of the
churches themselves. While encouraging such active participation within the churches, the new direction is to encourage the laity to discover what it means to be a Christian
at work in the world. This may be the new frontier in
developing a Christian impact on the vast systems in our
organized, complex, industrial society.

The laity is already in positions of leadership and membership in virtually every corporate structure. So the purpose of this book is to encourage and support the already
committed laity in their often lonely efforts to be effective

* RALPH D. BUCY is the pastor of the Good Shepherd Presbyterian Church in Houston, Texas. After twenty-five years in the
pastorate Mr. Bucy recognized his need to upgrade his pastoral
skills both by clinical experience and by academic inquiry. As
chaplain and graduate student at the University of Texas Medical
Branch in Galveston, he has studied philosophy, psychology, and
pastoral care. By mutual agreement with the Good Shepherd
Church, he is also a consultant to industry on moral issues. Having
accepted the challenge of *The New Laity* himself, Mr. Bucy is
appealing to both clergy and laity to grow in Christian effectiveness
in the world.

servants of the Lord where they already are. This book is addressed primarily to the laity and all people of good will—all the people of God.

The other major conviction which motivates the preparation of this book is that the people of God need to go beyond the first indispensable step of personal commitment to the Lord. The growth and development of the laity urgently requires some new skills and insight in discovering what it means to live and work in such a world as this.

One of the significant features of *The New Laity* is the wide variety and diversity of pluralistic traditions and backgrounds among its contributors. The ecumenical nature of its appeal is dramatically demonstrated by the writers who came from conservative evangelical Protestant churches, traditional Protestant churches, and the Roman Catholic Church. This is literally a new day in interchurch relationships and the laity is expressly seen as the leaders in such a new frontier of concern and caring for the whole human race.

This book grew out of a conference, "The Laity—A New Direction," held at the University of Dallas in June, 1976. The composition of the conference was almost equally representative of these three major clusters of Christian traditions. Five of the writers (Wedel, Mouw, Gremillion, Blake, and Swearingen), and the Editor (Bucy) participated in the conference. Six of the writers (Gillespie, Edge, J. Cunneen, S. Cunneen, Jaworski, and Shriver) were invited to write essays both because of their special talents and because, though not at the conference, their witness is a symbol of the expanding nature of the new direction.

In the time since the conference a great deal of thrilling new activity has taken place. You are invited to become part of the movement forward in developing this new direction, at a greater depth and in more intensive efforts to rediscover for yourself what it means for you to live and work in the world for Christ.

Biblical and
Theological
Foundations

Thomas W. Gillespie *

1.

The Laity in Biblical Perspective

WHEN PREVALENT ATTITUDES TOWARD the identity and ministry of the Christian laity are viewed in Biblical perspective, the necessity of "a new direction" becomes painfully evident.

The *direction* required involves movement that is both *upward* and *outward*—upward from an identity as second-class members of the community of faith to a status of full privilege and responsibility, and outward from a narrow preoccupation with the internal affairs of ecclesiastical institutions (church work) to a broad participation in the ministry of all members to the world (the work of the church).

By a *new* direction is meant a re*new*al of our present attitudes and commitments on the basis of a Biblical understanding of who the laity is and what the laity does. Such a renewal, because Biblically mandated, may be novel in the sense of unusual but not without precedent, original in the sense of returning to origins but not inven-

* THOMAS W. GILLESPIE is pastor of the First Presbyterian Church of Burlingame, California. He earned a Doctor's degree in Biblical studies at the Clairmont Cluster of theological schools.

tive, modern in the sense of contemporary but not innovative. It will manifest itself as a *fresh start* in the task that is endemic to the Christian community, as a *resumption* of the work that is inherent in the life of faith, as a *beginning again* of the mission that has been entrusted to believers from the very beginning.

IDENTIFYING THE LAITY

The clue to the identity of the laity is provided by the term itself—when Biblically defined. The qualification is necessary because of the devaluation of Biblical meaning in our vernacular use of the word. Today "the laity" signifies the secular notion of "nonprofessionals" in distinction from those who are specially trained or skilled, a concept derived from the religious idea of "ordinary believers" in distinction from those who are by training and office set apart as "clergy." It is this distinction between a lower and higher order, with the laity classified as the lower, that is foreign to the theological understanding of the laity in the Scriptures.

Having entered the English language by way of the Latin adjective *laicus,* a derivative of the Greek equivalent *laikos* (belonging to the people), the noun "laity" has its original source in the Greek word *laos* (people). In New Testament parlance *laos* frequently expresses an important theological concept, a concept inherited from the Septuagint, the Greek version of the Hebrew Old Testament. In the Septuagint *laos* is used with amazing consistency to translate the Hebrew word *am* (people), which itself is employed in the Old Testament almost exclusively as a designation of *Israel*. When non-Israelite peoples are mentioned in the Old Testament, the Hebrew text tends to use the term *goyim,* which the Septuagint renders by *ethne* (gentiles). In this close association with Israel, *laos* loses its general meaning of "crowd" or "population," and takes on the sense of a specific people, a people not in "mass" but in "union" because of the unique call of God. This people—Israel—is a special people precisely because of its origin and destiny in God's electing grace. Israel understands itself as *laos theou* (the people of God).

A classical expression of this self-understanding is set forth in Exodus 19:4–7. God says to Moses:

"You have seen what I did to the Egyptians, and how I bore you on eagles' wings and brought you to myself. Now therefore, if you will obey my voice and keep my covenant, you shall be my own possession among all peoples; for all the earth is mine, and you shall be to me a kingdom of priests and a holy nation. These are the words which you shall speak to the children of Israel."

So Moses came and called the elders of the people, and set before them all these words which the Lord had commanded him. And all the people answered together and said, "All that the Lord has spoken we will do." And Moses reported the words of the people to the Lord.

Notice that even though "the elders of the people" are mentioned here, the covenant is made with "all the people." The *laos* as a whole is God's "possession," chosen not for privilege alone but for the privilege of service. Notice also that the nature of this service is spelled out in direct connection with God's claim upon "all the earth." Israel is called from "among all the peoples" to serve as "a kingdom of priests and a holy nation" *in behalf of the kingdoms and nations of the world.* In this priestly service, Israel represents God to the world and the world to God. This people, the *laos* of God, is called, constituted, and commissioned to fulfill a mediating ministry.

So far as this ministry to the peoples of the earth is concerned, there is not the slightest justification in the terms of the covenant for that "split-level" distinction between "ordinary believer" and "clergy," between "novice" and "professional," which characterizes our contemporary use of the term "laity." On the contrary, our concept of the laity is altogether excluded by God's call to the entire *laos* to serve him as "a kingdom of priests." Even the later development of an official priesthood within Israel does not nullify this fundamental task of the people of God. For this later official priesthood always functions in a representative capacity for the entire *laos,* and its purpose is to enable the people as a whole to fulfill its priestly ministry to the world. Put simply, the laity of ancient Israel is composed of all who "belong to the people," to the people who belong to God. And the priestly service which constitutes obedience to God in the keeping of his covenant is the privilege and responsibility of the *laos* in its entirety.

It is this theological meaning of *laos* which passes from the Old Testament, by way of the Septuagint, into the New Testament when the term is used with reference to both the Israel of old and the new Israel, the Christian community (Gal. 6:16). The most remarkable affirmation of this continuity between the New Testament community of faith and that of the Old Testament is presented in the First Letter of Peter:

But you are a chosen race, a royal priesthood, a holy nation, God's own people, that you may declare the wonderful deeds of him who called you out of darkness into his marvelous light. Once you were no people but now you are God's people; once you had not received mercy but now you have received mercy (2:9,10).

Here the traditional titles of honor ascribed in the Old Testament to Israel as the *laos* of God are applied without reservation to the Christian community. What makes this affirmation remarkable is the fact that the titles are here ascribed to a community composed of both Jews and gentiles. Those who were once "no people" but who are now "God's people" are the gentile Christians. In Christ the radical distinction and separation between the *laos* and the *ethne,* between Israel and the gentiles, has been transcended. The circle of membership in the people of God is now drawn from a new center—Jesus Christ, the Lord and

Savior of the world. Through the gospel God has called
all people "out of darkness into his marvelous light." And
all who respond to his call in faith are numbered among
those who now "have received mercy" (cf. also the apostle
Paul's similar affirmation in Romans 9:24–26).

The titles of honor, however, make it plain that membership in the Christian community is not an honorary position. For explicit in the titles is the task which they
mandate. And this task, again specified as a priestly service,
is given as before to the *laos* in general and to its members
in particular. Whatever the leadership roles within this
priestly community may be (and the New Testament at-
tests to a great variety), the fact remains that here, as in
Exodus 19:4–7, the priesthood and its responsibilities are
assigned to the whole *laos*. As in ancient Israel, so also in
the new Israel the laity are those who "belong to the people," to the people who belong to God, to the God who in
Jesus Christ calls them to a mediating ministry in behalf
of the world.

This is the new *upward* direction which a Biblical perspective on the laity requires of us—the elevation of every
member of God's people to the status of a minister. The renewal of a Biblically informed theological identity of the
laity, however, must not be construed as a call for the
"clericalization" of the entire Christian community. In
fact, the need to guard against such a misunderstanding is
indicative of the confusion about the ministry of the *laos*
of God which the distinction between "clergy" and "laity"
has fostered since its evolvement from the third century
onwards.

The so-called "clergy," themselves members of the *laos,*
have their own special ministry within the priestly community. And this ministry enjoys ample Biblical warrant.
But when it is identified as "the ministry" of the community itself, as has been the tendency within the history
of the church, the result is a theological disaster. For the
laos then delegates the ministry, primarily if not exclu-

sively, to the "clergy," and relegates the "laity" (now understood as nonclergy) to the role of a "supporting cast." Further, this identification of the ministry of the *laos* with the special ministry of the *kleros* ("clergy") also introverts the direction of the ministry of God's people. For the ministry of the "clergy" is directed predominantly *to* the community itself, with the result that the ministry *of* the community to the world is shamefully neglected. The ministry inevitably becomes self-serving, directed *inward* toward the development and preservation of individual faith and institutional health.

As important as these matters are, they are important only for the sake of the vitality and sensitivity of the community's ministry to the world. Only if and when the *laos* as a whole discovers and recovers its identity as a priesthood unto God for the sake of a mediating ministry to the world will its service become genuinely extroverted and thereby authenticated. Then the respective roles of the "laity" and "clergy" will be reversed, with the former taking the lead in their daily interface with the society at large and the latter supporting this primary and priority ministry of the people of God through their special ministry of the Word and the Sacraments. It is this outward direction of the ministry of the *laos* which is mandated by its identity as "a chosen race, a royal priesthood, a holy nation, God's own people."

THE MINISTRY OF THE LAITY

The vision of a priestly ministry turned *outward* to the world may seem at first contradictory because of our common association of a priesthood with cultic duties performed in the service of a sanctuary. The term *priest* conjures up images of people engaged with sacred objects in sacred places far removed, ideologically if not geographically, from the intersections of daily life. Priestly service suggests withdrawal from the world rather than involvement in it. Certainly the priesthood as practiced in the history of religions justifies this impression. Even the Old Testament priesthood within Israel falls into this pattern. Yet the Christian community should remember that in Jesus Christ the priesthood of the *laos* of God has been radically redefined.

This redefinition is intimated in 1 Peter, in the same passage in which "God's own people" are identified as "a royal priesthood." Preceding this identification, the readers of the letter are exhorted, "Come to him, to that living stone, rejected by men but in God's sight chosen and precious; and like living stones be yourselves built into a spiritual house, to be a holy priesthood, to offer spiritual sacrifices acceptable to God through Jesus Christ" (1 Peter 2:4,5). The operative words in this exhortation are "through Jesus Christ." The meaning of temple, priesthood, and sacrifice is here predicated upon the redemptive ministry of Jesus, a predication which results in a thoroughgoing reinterpretation of all three concepts.

1. *Temple*

It is affirmed in these verses that the risen Christ is "that living stone" who forms around himself "a spiritual house" composed of those who by faith in him are themselves "like living stones." The sanctuary of God on earth is here redefined as "the Christian community" itself. Through Jesus Christ the sacred place is replaced by the sacred people, the "holy nation," the *laos* of God's own possession. The same understanding appears in the Pauline correspondence within the New Testament. "Do you not know that you are God's temple and that God's Spirit dwells in you?" Paul asks the Corinthian congregation (1 Cor. 3:16). What is true of the community is equally true of its members. In the same letter the apostle inquires of individual believers, "Do you not know that your body is a temple of the Holy Spirit within you, which you have from God?" (6:19). And in the letter to the Ephesians it is declared that the household of God is "built upon the foundation of the apostles and prophets, Christ Jesus himself being the cornerstone, in whom the whole structure is joined together and grows into a holy temple in the Lord; in whom you also are built into it for a dwelling place of God in the Spirit" (Eph. 2:20–22). Such passages clearly indicate the radical redefinition of the temple concept which has been introduced "through Jesus Christ." God's "dwelling place" on earth is no longer conceived of as a building set apart from the world, but as a people set in and sent unto the world.

The worldward thrust of this reinterpretation is enjoined by the dominical mandates under which the temple-community lives. "Go therefore and make disciples of all nations" (Matt. 28:19). "As the Father has sent me, even so I send you" (John 20:21). "You shall be my witnesses in Jerusalem and in all Judea and Samaria and to the end of the earth" (Acts 1:8). Because the gospel of redemption is intended for the world of creation, the temple takes on global proportions as the Christian community fulfills its global task. In the fulfillment of the Christian community's ministry to the world, the people of God who are honored as "a people of his possession" (1 Peter 2:9) themselves honor his claim that "all the earth is mine" (Ex. 19:5). With the psalmist the temple-people confess, "The earth is the Lord's and the fulness thereof, the world and those who dwell therein" (Ps. 24:1). The temple is now a mission engaged in the task of reclaiming the world for God and renewing human life through the power of the Holy Spirit, whom it bears and by whom it is itself borne. And it does so in the horizon hope of a "new heaven and a new earth," in the confident expectation of "the holy city, new Jerusalem, coming down out of heaven from God." When this hope is realized, then it will be said, "Behold, the dwelling of God is with men. He will dwell with them, and they shall be his people, and God himself will be with them" (Rev. 21:1–3). In the seer's vision of this city of God's ultimate future there is no temple, "for its temple is the Lord God the Almighty and the Lamb" (Rev. 21:22).

Undergirding and informing the worldward mission of God's temple-people is his world-wide love. "For God so loved the world that he gave his only Son" (John 3:16). The giving of his Son is not only motivated by God's love for the world, but his love for the world is manifested in the giving of his Son. "In this the love of God was made manifest among us, that God sent his only Son into the world, so that we might live through him" (1 John 4:9). The pronouns "us" and "we" in this text certainly include the Christian community, but they do not exclude the world. For "the Father has sent his Son as the Savior of the world" (1 John 4:14). The Savior comes to the world in the "flesh" (John 1:14), to the world that needs saving, to the world in all its complicity and culpability, in all its duplicity and mendacity. In the flesh he lives out the love of God that is grace—love for the unloved, the unlovely, and the unlovable; love that is unearned, undeserved, and unmerited. His living of grace is his obedience to the Father who sent him, an obedience "unto death, even death on a cross" (Phil. 2:8). Indeed, "God shows his love for us in that while we were yet sinners Christ died for us" (Rom. 5:8). The temple-people of God experiences this love in the heart (Rom. 5:5), and lives under its control (2 Cor. 5:14). In its mission to the world the beloved people is moved by the same love for the world which sent its Lord into the world. It takes up "the ministry of reconciliation" because "God was in Christ reconciling the world to himself" (2 Cor. 5:18–19).

The New Testament reinterpretation of the temple concept has profound consequences for our understanding of the popular distinction between sacred and secular spheres of life. God's temple-presence as a people-presence means that the profane (from the Latin *profanus,* meaning "be-

fore the temple") recedes before the advance of the community in its ministry to the world. Because God is where
his people are, corporately or individually, wherever they
are becomes a sacred place. Every activity of this people in the world, whether public or private, business or
pleasure, labor or leisure, social or political, is a religious
activity. For religion is understood by this people as life
that is lived before God in faith. There is no domain within
the various dimensions of God's good creation which are
by definition "off limits" or "out of bounds" to the people
of God. The world of economics and politics, of medicine
and law, of art and music, of management and labor, of
education and research, is the proper sphere of sacred
service.

THE "CALLING" OF THE LAITY

The vulnerability of the secular to the sacred, of the
profane world to the temple-people, gives strategic importance to the Biblical doctrine of *vocation* (calling).
The God who dwells in and among his people on earth is
the One who calls us "in the grace of Christ" (Gal. 1:6;
cf. 1:15) to the blessings of salvation. His summons is
variously described in the New Testament as a call to his
kingdom and glory (1 Thess. 2:12), to the fellowship of
his Son (1 Cor. 1:9), to peace (1 Cor. 7:15; cf. Col.
3:15), to freedom (Gal. 5:13), to hope (Eph. 4:4), to
holiness (1 Thess. 4:7; cf. 2 Thess. 2:13–14), to eternal
life (1 Tim. 6:12), to his eternal glory in Christ (1 Peter
5:10; cf. 2 Peter 1:3), to the marriage supper of the Lamb
(Rev. 19:9). Each facet of the salvation to which the
Christian community is called through the gospel, however,
represents both a gift to be enjoyed and a task to be performed. The salvation received in faith is to be expressed
in life. It becomes evident in the world by its ethical yield.
Christians are exhorted, accordingly, "to lead a life worthy
of the calling to which you have been called" (Eph. 4:1).

The ethical imperative implicit in the vocation of the people of God is particularly evident in his call to holiness (1 Thess. 4:7). Biblically understood, holiness is the status of those who have been "set apart" for God. It is a status conferred from above rather than achieved from below. The temple-community is "a holy nation" because it is "God's own people" (1 Peter 2:9). Members of this community are designated throughout the New Testament as "saints" (holy ones). Even the Corinthian Christians, for all of their questionable behavior, are addressed as "those sanctified in Christ Jesus, called to be saints together with all those who in every place call on the name of our Lord Jesus Christ, both their Lord and ours" (1 Cor. 1:2). Yet it is clear that the status conferred by God's grace is a status to be confirmed by holy living. "As obedient children, do not be conformed to the passions of your former ignorance, but as he who called you is holy, be holy yourselves in all your conduct; since it is written, 'You shall be holy, for I am holy' " (1 Peter 1:14–16, citing the Priestly Code from Lev. 11:44–45). God's temple-people have been "called . . . out of darkness into his marvelous light" (1 Peter 2:9).

This "calling," let it be emphasized, is not "out of the world" but out of the spiritual and moral darkness which envelopes the world. It is a "calling" into the spiritual and moral light which is given to the world in Jesus Christ ("I am the light of the world," John 9:5), and which his disciples are to reflect in the world ("You are the light of the world," Matt. 5:14). It is not assumed in the New Testament that living the light of Jesus Christ is an easy task. On the contrary, those who "do right and suffer for it" patiently have God's approval, for "to this you have been called" (1 Peter 2:20–21). Under persecution believers are instructed, "Do not return evil for evil or reviling for reviling; but on the contrary bless, for to this you have been called, that you may obtain a blessing" (1 Peter 3:9).

Yet in spite of the cost, it is in the fulfilling of its voca-

tion—the divine "calling" to live out the salvation of God
—that the temple-people brings the sacred to the secular
world. The "holy nation" brings holiness to the profane
precincts of life which stand "before the temple," not
merely by its presence in the world but by its obedience to
the God who claims the world for himself.

The nature and scope of this "calling" make it plain that
it is the vocation of all believers. Each member of the *laos*
stands under God's call, and each is accountable for his
or her response to it. In no way is this negated or com-
promised by the manner in which Paul speaks of himself
as "called to be an apostle" (Rom. 1:1; 1 Cor. 1:1; cf.
Gal. 1:1). The call of God is indeed individualized and
particularized in concrete tasks, and Paul's apostleship is
a prime example of this. But it may not be used to justify
the view stemming from medieval times that only the
"clergy" have a "calling" from God. Vocation is the gift
and task of the whole people of God, enjoyed and exercised
in that concrete corner of the world in which the individual
member lives. Paul himself confirms this in a significant
passage from 1 Corinthians. "Only," he writes, "let every
one lead the life which the Lord has assigned to him, and
in which God has called him" (7:17). This "rule," which
is said to apply to all of the apostle's churches, is then
restated in slightly different language: "Every one should
remain in the state (calling) in which he was called"
(7:20). Here "the life which the Lord has assigned" is
interpreted as a "calling," referring to the life-situation of
the individual at the time of God's call to faith.

This interpretation of the believer's place in life as a
"calling" is made not only possible but necessary by the
claim of God upon the full scope of human existence, the entire range of human activities. Because of God's call the
believer's life-situation becomes the place where responsibility for this "calling" is fulfilled. Included in this claim
is certainly the believer's occupation. For God's call trans-
forms our life work. No longer is it simply the way in

which we earn a living. Now it is the place in the world
in which we give expression to the Christian life. In exhort-
ing his readers to "remain" in the situation in which God
calls them, Paul is not urging upon them a kind of vocational immobility. He is rather encouraging them to bloom
where they are planted, to honor God's claim upon their
life in the world, and to work that claim in his behalf.
"So, brethren," he concludes, "in whatever state each was
called, there let him remain *with God*" (7:24).

A more radical reinterpretation of the traditional temple
concept is difficult to imagine. God's "dwelling" upon earth
is a people rather than a building, a holy people "set apart"
for God rather than from the world, a people mandated to
mission rather than coddled in seclusion, a people called
by God to the living of salvation in the matrix of everyday
life rather than delivered from life's cares and responsibilities, a people who live "before God" at all times and
in all places rather than lead double lives in segregated
sacred and secular compartments. Ministry in such a temple-community can only be worldward in its thrust.

2. *Priesthood*

According to 1 Peter, the new temple-people is formed
also by the risen Christ "to be a holy priesthood" (2:5).
Given the reinterpretation of the temple concept "through
Jesus Christ," it is not surprising that a similar transformation of meaning occurs in the New Testament with regard
to the priesthood familiar to the people of God from the
Old Testament. This redefinition is the primary intention
of the letter to the Hebrews.

The theme of this unique New Testament document is
"Jesus, the apostle and high priest of our confession"
(3:1). He is set forth as "a merciful and faithful high priest
in the service of God" (2:17), as "a great high priest who
has passed through the heavens" (4:14), as "a high priest
for ever" (6:20). In ancient Israel the high priest was

"called by God" (5:4), and "appointed to act on behalf
of men in relation to God, to offer gifts and sacrifices for
sins" (5:1; cf. 8:3). The office was established as "the order
of Aaron" (7:11), the first high priest, and was tradi-
tionally filled by a descendant of Levi. To this office, according to the bold claim of the anonymous author of
Hebrews, Christ has now been "appointed" (5:5; cf.
3:1–2), in fulfillment of the messianic promise of Psalm
110:4 (5:6), "designated by God a high priest after the
order of Melchizedek" (Heb. 5:10), that mysterious priest
without known predecessor or successor to whom the
patriarch Abraham rendered an offering in Genesis 14:17–
20 (7:1–10).

This transfer of the high priesthood from "the order of
Aaron" to "the order of Melchizedek" (7:11), from the
tribe of Levi to the Messiah of Israel, represents "a change
in the priesthood" effected by "a change in the law"
(7:12). The "former commandment is set aside because
of its weakness and uselessness" (7:18), and in its place
is established "a better covenant" (7:22), "a new covenant" that renders the first "obsolete" (8:13).

In his high priestly role, Jesus is the mediator of this new
covenant (9:15; 13:24; cf. 8:6). By definition a mediator
is an intermediary, a "man in the middle," a "go-between,"
an agent of reconciliation. As one who seeks to reestablish
broken relationships, a mediator must have the trust of the
parties at variance. This trust is frequently based upon the
neutrality of the mediator, upon the fact of his belonging
to neither side. The most effective mediator, however, is
one who represents both parties, who belongs to both sides,
who is involved with all concerned. Such is the high priest,
according to Hebrews, who mediates God's new covenant
with humankind. This high priest is "Jesus, the Son of
God" (4:14), the Son who is God's Word to the world
(1:2), who "reflects the glory of God and bears the very
stamp of his nature" (1:3). Yet, at the same time, he is
the high priest who is unashamed to call us "brethren"

(2:11), who in sharing our "flesh and blood" partakes of our nature (2:14), who is made like us "in every respect" (2:17), who has suffered and been tempted (2:18), yet without sinning (4:15). It is this identification with us and this obedience to God which qualifies him as "a merciful and faithful high priest in the service of God" (2:17), making "intercession" always for us (7:25), and appearing "in the presence of God on our behalf" (9:24).

The high priesthood of Jesus is the foundation of the "holy priesthood" which belongs to the people of God (1 Peter 2:4). Each member of the Christian community is authorized "through Jesus Christ" to exercise personally the priestly privilege of direct access to God. The high priesthood of Jesus invites believers into the sphere of "immediacy" in their relationship with God. Hebrews speaks of "a new and living way" into God's presence which the high priest over God's house has opened to us (10:20,21), and exhorts us to "draw near with a true heart in full assurance of faith" (10:22). And again, "Let us then with confidence draw near to the throne of grace, that we may receive mercy and find grace to help in time of need" (4:16).

The vital importance of this individual "drawing near" to God through Christ must not be depreciated in reaction to its inherent danger of degenerating into pious individualism. For the direct access of the believer to God, the immediate contact of human faith with divine grace, is the basis of both spiritual freedom and ethical responsibility. It is in the intimacy of "drawing near" that the believer makes ultimate decisions "before God," decisions which affect the life and destiny of human relationships and institutions. Further, authentic priestly ministry is not exercised merely in one's own behalf. It is a service also rendered in behalf of others, of all others. A priesthood without a people to represent, to pray for, to intercede for, is superfluous. In 1 Peter the "holy priesthood" (2:4) is also called the "royal priesthood" (2:9), meaning "the

King's priests." As a priesthood "set apart" for God, it
ministers under his sovereign claim upon the whole world.
This is the God the priesthood represents to the world, the
God who claims the world for himself. And this is the world
the priesthood represents to God, the world that stub-
bornly denies his claim.

The model for this priestly ministry is Jesus, the mediator
of the new covenant. Believers are not mediators in themselves. "For there is one God, and there is one mediator
between God and men, the man Christ Jesus" (1 Tim.
2:5). Yet, as men and women who are "in Christ," believers are included in the ministry of the "one mediator."
And his earthly style of identification with the world in
obedience to God is normative for all who serve him. As
the high priest shared our humanity, our temptations, and
our sufferings, so the priestly people of God participate
fully in the conditions and situations of life in the world.
The priesthood of Jesus Christ does not stand "above it
all" but "in the midst of it all." Yet standing with the world
does not mean going along with the world. Identification
with humanity does not involve capitulation to its understanding of humanness. On the contrary, the priestly presence of the people of God is a presence with a difference.
And this difference translates out in terms of obedience to
God from within the very structures of life in the world
in which he is so commonly denied.

It is evident then that the priesthood also has been redefined "through Jesus Christ." The provisional Levitical
priesthood of the old covenant has been supplanted by a
new covenant in which Jesus serves as the permanent high
priest of the people of God. Every member of the new covenant community participates officially in its priesthood,
enjoying both direct access to God through Christ and a
mediating ministry before God in behalf of the world. In
its position between God and the world, between the world
and God, the priesthood of all believers is postured both
Godward and worldward. And it models its ministry after

its high priest, who identified himself with the world in order to offer obedience to God in the world. It is to this offering that our attention must now turn.

3. *Sacrifice*

The task of the "holy priesthood" which the risen Christ forms about himself as "a spiritual house" is defined in 1 Peter as the offering of "spiritual sacrifices acceptable to God through Jesus Christ" (2:5). The qualification of "sacrifices" as "spiritual" indicates that here, too, a reinterpretation of a central cultic concept in the Old Testament is presented. The occasion for this reinterpretation is the death of Jesus, which the New Testament understands as sacrificial in character and atoning in significance. Paul speaks of "the redemption which is in Christ Jesus, whom God put forward as an expiation by his blood, to be received by faith" (Rom. 3:24,25). First John declares that "we have an advocate with the Father, Jesus Christ the righteous; and he is the expiation for our sins, and not for ours only but also for the sins of the whole world" (2:1,2). Again, "In this is love, not that we loved God but that he loved us and sent his Son to be the expiation for our sins" (4:10).

The theme of expiation of sins through sacrificial death is developed most fully, however, by the letter to the Hebrews. Here it is affirmed that the primary task of Jesus the high priest is "to make expiation for the sins of the people" (2:17). This he accomplished not by continuing the sacrificial prescriptions of the Mosaic law, which were provisional because inherently inadequate (7:11; 9:9–10; 10:1–4), but by the offering of himself (7:27), indeed, "by the sacrifice of himself" (9:26). In offering himself to God in behalf of the people, Jesus sacrificed his life—a life perfected by victory over temptation (4:15) through obedience in suffering (5:8,9; cf. 7:28).

Unlike the high priests under the Levitical code, who

were compelled to offer sacrifices for their own sins as well as those of the people (7:27; 9:7), the new high priest is "holy, blameless, unstained, separated from sinners" (7:26). Thus he "offered himself without blemish to God" (9:14) when he "endured the cross, despising the shame" (12:2). In his crucifixion he tasted death for everyone "by the grace of God" (2:9), and through death destroyed him who has the power of death (2:14), thereby delivering all who through fear of death were in lifelong bondage (2:15). On the cross he bore the sins of many (9:28), effected the forgiveness of sins (9:22), and purified our conscience from dead works to serve the living God (9:14; cf. 10:10–14). In his resurrection and exaltation he "entered once for all into the Holy Place, taking not the blood of goats and calves but his own blood, thus securing an eternal redemption" (9:12). Accordingly, his sacrifice is both singular (10:12–14) and "once for all" (7:27; 9:12,26,28; 10:11). His offering stands "for all time a single sacrifice for sins" (10:12).

The one sacrifice of Christ does not eliminate the necessity of further sacrifices by believers. It does, however, radically change their character and purpose. In a concluding exhortation, the author of Hebrews himself suggests this change. "Through him then let us continually offer up a sacrifice of praise to God, that is, the fruit of lips that acknowledge his name. Do not neglect to do good and to share what you have, for such sacrifices are pleasing to God" (13:15,16). The term "then" indicates that the author is here speaking of a consequence which necessarily follows from the sacrificial offering of Jesus. Christian sacrifices are not an addition to the atoning death of the new high priest of God's people, for his perfect offering is without need of supplementation. Rather they are responses to his redemptive work, responses of praise and thanksgiving, of personal confession and loving service, all of which are mediated "through him." They are the words and deeds of love which answer to the love manifested in the sacrifice of Christ. "And walk in love," the Ephesians are exhorted, "as Christ loved us and gave himself up for us, a fragrant offering and sacrifice to God" (Eph. 5:2).

Such sacrifices, however, are the outward expression of that deep and total offering of human life to God which the apostle Paul designates as the only logical response to God's redeeming grace in Christ. "I appeal to you therefore, brethren, by the mercies of God, to present your bodies as a living sacrifice, holy and acceptable to God, which is your spiritual worship" (Rom. 12:1). By "body" Paul means the corporeal existence of the individual, the concrete portion of God's creation which a human being represents, including the full range of his or her activities, involvements, and influences in the world. Worship of this kind obviously may not be limited to acts of private and corporate devotion. It embraces the duties and responsibilities, the opportunities and possibilities of everyday life. Its liturgy is literally "the work of the people" in the workaday world. Offering our bodies as living sacrifices in response to God's grace means placing our lives at God's disposal and in his service "lock, stock, and barrel."

From this depth of life commitment flow the words and deeds of Christian sacrifice. And neither form of sacrifice may be legitimately emphasized or neglected at the expense of the other. For when "the Word became flesh" (John 1:14), the marriage of word and deed was permanently consummated. Paul thus ventures to speak of what Christ has worked through him "by word and deed" in his ministry to the gentiles (Rom. 15:18). Proclamation and demonstration belong together as components of a single obedience in his "priestly service of the gospel of God," and the fruit of faith which this "stereo" service effects in human life is an "offering" to God (Rom. 15:16; cf. Phil. 2:17).

Likewise the priestly ministry of God's laity requires a willingness to "show and tell" the good news of his love for the world. In this ministry there is no place for "closet

Christians." It demands public sacrifices of personal obedience to Christ on the altar of life's daily affairs. These are the "spiritual sacrifices" of the "holy priesthood" which are "acceptable to God through Jesus Christ" (1 Peter 2:5), sacrifices that are wrought by the Spirit, mediated by the Son, and offered in grateful response to God's redeeming grace.

Even this brief review of the reinterpretation by the New Testament of the cultic concepts of temple, priesthood, and sacrifice inherited from the Old Testament makes it sufficiently evident that the ministry of the laity of God is directed outward to the world. God's temple-people go forth into the world under orders, recognizing no artificial distinctions between sacred and secular spheres of sovereignty, living salvation in the place of their individual calling, invading the precincts of the profane under the banner of God's claim upon all the earth. God's "royal priesthood" serves him in the world beneath the high priesthood of Christ, enjoying direct access to the divine presence, using that access to intercede for the world with which it has identified itself in obedience to the model of the earthly ministry of Jesus. In grateful response to the atoning death of Christ, the people of God's own possession offer their individual lives in all of their actuality as living sacrifices, and express his life commitment in the daily sacrifices of word and deed which are "pleasing" to God because they bear witness to his love and purpose for the world.

This then is the "new direction" which a Biblical perspective on the Christian laity requires of us today. It calls for a widespread recognition and honoring of the Biblical vision of the unity of the *laos* of God, of the ministry of all members, of the priesthood of all believers, of the vocation of all Christians. It will be realized only if the "nonclergy" are willing to move up, if the "clergy" are willing to move over, and if all God's people are willing to move out. For the ministry of this community is rendered first and foremost in the world and for the world. It is performed in the daily lives of its people, in their participation and involvement in the structures of a complex society, in their sacrificial obedience in "worldly affairs," in their mission to reclaim the world for the God who claims the world for himself in love.

Cynthia C. Wedel *

2.

A World-wide Vision
of Church and World

"GOD SO LOVED THE WORLD THAT HE GAVE
his only Son, that whoever believes in him should not
perish, but have eternal life. For God sent the Son into
the world, not to condemn the world, but that the world
might be saved through him" (John 3:16,17).

This is God's world. He made it. He loves it. He put us
and the church in the world to save the world. This is the
overwhelming challenge we face. Yet many people today
are discouraged and hopeless about the world in which we
live. Threats and problems seem insolvable, and the human
reaction is to retreat into our own small circles of home,
community, and local congregation. We Christians claim
to be followers—disciples—of Jesus. His early disciples
spent much time with their Lord, learning from his words
and his example, as we should do in our corporate and

* DR. CYNTHIA C. WEDEL is president of the World Council of
Churches, and makes her home in Alexandria, Virginia. She is a
gracious lady, a warm and genuine human being. She was the first
president of the National Council of Churches and one of the first
two women to be elected president of the WCC. She is also National Chairman of Volunteers, American Red Cross.

private worship and Bible study. But his disciples were changed by their experience with him from simple, ordinary folk into joyous, fearless people who went out into the world preaching, teaching, and healing. Most of them became martyrs, but they changed the world.

We live in a world as cruel and oppressive as the world of two thousand years ago. It is a world which needs the basic Christian message that God cares, as much as it was needed then. Men and women who have learned that God does care—that God is love and is all-powerful—could once again turn the world upside down. Many modern church people talk and act as though God were dead, or had at least resigned some time ago and left his world to its own destruction. But we, who are part of God's church, who have read our Bibles, know that the God of the Bible, the God who is the father of our Lord Jesus Christ, is not dead. He is the one who said, "Lo, I am with you always, even to the end of the age." The God we know and worship is a living, loving, active God, constantly pushing and pulling us toward that which he wills for us.

One problem is, of course, that God made us free. As far as we know, we are the only part of the created world to which God gave real freedom of choice. Unlike rocks or plants or animals, we are not limited to obeying built-in instincts. We can choose what we will or will not do. We can say yes or no even to our Creator. Many people deny this and insist that we are bound by our heredity or our environment. But we know—deep in our hearts—that this is not so. We make choices and decisions a hundred or a thousand times every day. These may be influenced by outward forces, but each of us has the power to make his or her own decisions.

When we consider the implications of human freedom, we may wonder why God did such a foolish thing. He could just as easily have made us so that we would have to behave in certain ways. And think what a lovely place this world would be if every human being always did what was right and loving and kind! What could he have wanted even more than he wanted a peaceful, pleasant universe?

My guess is that, since the Bible says that God *is* love (not that he loves, but that love is his essential nature), God wanted to create love in his universe. But how do you create love? It isn't something you can make, like a rock or a flower. Love is a relationship. God realized that the only way to create love was to create a being with whom he could have a love relationship. And God knew that love must always be a free gift. If there is any element of force or coercion, you may get a reasonable facsimile of love, but it will not be the perfect love which is freely given.

The truth of this can be seen in human relationships. When slavery was practiced in many parts of the world, it was often said that masters loved their slaves, and slaves loved their masters. And there were, undoubtedly, many fine relationships between masters and slaves. Yet, how can you know? If one person has the power of life and death over another, the slave will avoid expressing hatred or resentment. The same thing happened in many marriages. When women had almost no choice but to marry, there were probably many extremely unhappy marriages. But a woman, trapped in a loveless marriage, could only pretend to a loving relationship. She had no way out. But real love is love between equals, where each is an independent autonomous human being and chooses to live in relationship with the other. This could be one of the fruits of the growing freedom of women in our time.

Knowing of the need for equality and freedom as a basis for love, God evidently decided to take the risk of creating a being "in his own image"—free as God is free—in order to have one with whom a love relationship would be possible. Obviously, God knew that his human children would try out their freedom—as in the story of Adam and Eve.

They would disobey their Creator, and perhaps even use their freedom to deny his existence. But God evidently decided that it was worth the risk and limited himself to wooing and trying to win the love of his creatures.

This is reflected over and over again in the Bible. Like a loving parent, God acts. He does good things for his human children, gives them a lovely garden in which to live, rescues them from slavery, leads them to a promised land, and eventually comes and lives among them in human form to try to show his love for them. And over and over again human beings disobey, turn against God's wishes, and finally put him to death. Yet even this final rebellion—the crucifixion of Jesus—cannot end God's love. In the glorious story of Easter, the resurrection, God shows that his love is everlasting.

The little band of disciples who had known and loved Jesus, even though they turned traitor at the time of the crucifixion, finally realized after the resurrection that the man Jesus, whom they had come to love, was actually the almighty Creator of heaven and earth in human form. And this realization transformed them from weak, frightened creatures into loving, courageous people who went out and conquered the world of their time with the triumphant message that "God cares."

BUT WE ARE FEARFUL

This is the message for which every human heart hungers. We human beings are fundamentally fearful, unsure of ourselves, afraid of others. We all want to be liked, to be well thought of. We constantly compare ourselves with others, and we can always find someone who is wiser or stronger or more fortunate than we are. An inferiority complex is an almost universal human trait. A wise theologian once said that an inferiority complex is a form of original sin. It is doubting God, implying that God didn't know what he was doing when he made us. Otherwise he would have made us brighter or richer or whatever characteristic we most desire. But when we begin to develop a real faith in God, we realize that God does not make mistakes. He made each of us as we are because he wants us this way. He has something which he wants each of us to do. If we would learn to trust him and to use whatever gifts he gave us—however small—in his service to our fellow human beings, we might begin to be the confident, hopeful, effective people God meant us to be.

It is interesting in this connection to think about the great saints of Christian tradition. Few of them, including Jesus' disciples, were unusual people. Most of them were simple folk, almost never rich or powerful or brilliant. Their one common quality was that they had come to really trust God, to believe "in" God to the extent of doing whatever they felt God was calling them to do. And their lives and words and deeds are remembered through all of history.

We modern Christians need more than anything else to work toward a deeper understanding of the God in whom we say we believe. We need to read our Bibles, meditate, pray, and talk together about our faith. We need to grow beyond the childish notions of God which so many adults retain. Above all, we need to stretch our finite human minds and realize that God is far greater than we are. Someone has said that God made man in his own image, and man has been returning the compliment ever since. Or, as J. B. Phillips said in the title of one of his books: "Your God Is Too Small." We need to try to grasp the fact that God is, indeed, the Creator of heaven and earth (and becoming more amazing as modern science extends the size of the universe); that God is still ruling the universe; that he is a good and loving and infinitely patient God. Above all, we need to recognize that God has chosen us, his human children, to carry out his will for his creation.

Once we begin to comprehend this, all kinds of things become clear. There is a good and loving purpose in the universe and in history. Because of the self-centeredness of human beings this good purpose is constantly thwarted. Those who gain power or wealth use it for their own ends and not for the good of others. But in spite of all the bad things in history and in the world today those who believe in and trust God know that there is great hope. Because God made us free and will not violate our freedom by intervening directly in the course of human history, he makes use of individuals and of the events of history to point the way. And one can imagine God hoping that some people will discern, in the things which he makes possible, his plans and the way he wants things to be.

THE IMPACT OF SCIENCE

We are living in one of the periods in history when God is showing us many signs of the future. The great question is—will we see his hand in the events of our time and begin to work with and not against him? We can look back a century or two and see how in many different places God began to let people discover secrets of the universe which he had created but which had been hidden until then. Out of these discoveries came modern science, and from science the technology was developed which has changed the world so drastically.

Think, for example, of how the world has shrunk within the past century. As late as 1900, the world to most people was still a vast and largely unknown place. People lived in small, homogeneous communities. Most of us knew little of what happened beyond our own small village or neighborhood. It was a constricted and narrow life, but reasonably peaceful and undisturbed. But think of the contrast of today, when we can be on the other side of the world in a few hours or can sit in our comfortable living rooms and watch, in living color, events taking place in remote lands. War, famine, and disasters become almost daily fare.

Many people react to this by wondering why, in our time, so many awful things happen. They forget that these things have always happened, but in the past we didn't know about them. The vast world has shrunk into a little global village in which we all live close together and are aware of problems never recognized before. At the same time we are coming to know much more about other people. As we see people of a different nation or race in their poverty or suffering, we are beginning to realize that they suffer as we do, enjoy and want what we do, and are basically just like us.

Knowledge of all the events of the world is very disturbing and uncomfortable. Life can never again be as peaceful as it once was. But what do you think God may have in mind? I suspect that from the day of creation, God wanted his beloved human children to live together on this lovely planet in peace and brotherhood, sharing the good things of the earth and caring for our common inheritance and for one another. But this has never been possible until now. For the first time in human history you and I are living when it is possible to imagine a world of mutual understanding, peace, and brotherhood. God's gifts to us of modern science and technology make this possible. The question is—will we see the hope in it and put our skill and energy to work for the family of humankind, or will we continue to be hung up in our old national and racial fears and rivalries?

As another example of God's activity, think of how threatened many middle-class Americans are by the uprisings and revolutions which are going on in our world. We see formerly submissive and "peaceful" colonial lands demanding—and winning—their independence. Racial minorities are rising up and demanding freedom and a share in the decision making which affects them. Young people have been rebelling against the authority of home and school. And belatedly women have joined the fight for liberation. What a contrast to the "good old days" when everyone knew his place and stayed in it!

THE SPREAD OF EDUCATION

These changes, too, stem largely from technology. As people began to learn how others live, those who had very little raised questions of "why?" Education has spread rapidly throughout the world in the past century. (It is important to remember that Christian missionaries had a large share in this.) And, in addition to formal education, the spread of information, especially by radio, to remote villages everywhere has helped to raise the consciousness and the aspirations of people. As the oppressed and deprived of the world—the great majority of mankind—learned that others had a life very different from theirs, they began to ask why and to demand their share of freedom, self-determination, and prosperity.

In a very human reaction, the nations and people who had wealth and power, often built on the labor and resources of the deprived, generally resisted demands for change and brought on rebellion and strife. Ours is an uncomfortable time. But as Christians we need to ask, "What does God want?" We believe that God made and loves all of his human children. He cannot have been happy with a world in which a small proportion of people had almost all the wealth and power while the majority had no freedom and only a marginal standard of living. Surely God wants every one of his human children to have a chance to be fully human, to have freedom, dignity, and a decent life. And, once again, we are living in the first period in human history when this might be possible. Economists and scientists tell us that if even a fraction of what the developed nations now spend on armaments and luxuries were used to help the developing nations and the poor and unemployed everywhere, human dignity and prosperity could be shared with the entire world with no negative economic consequences. If Christian people, striving to discern God's hand in the events of our time, can begin to see the hope which is present even in some of the frightening happenings of today and can catch a vision of what it means to join with our Creator in working out his purposes, nothing can stop us.

What do we need to do? First, many of us need to realize that we probably don't know as much as we should about our faith and about God. The average adult American Christian, who may be highly educated in general knowledge and in a profession, usually has about a fifth-grade understanding of theology. We have fallen into the fallacy of assuming that theology is something for the clergy. But theology is "talking about God," and we all can and need to do this. Theology is no longer confined to theological seminaries or to large, formidable volumes. It appears in magazines and books which are easily read by lay people. As intelligent lay men and women, we need to stop depending on someone else—the clergy usually—to "educate" us, and we must not blame them because we do not understand the Bible or theology. If we want to learn anything else, a foreign language or how to repair an automobile, we are quite capable of finding a class, or starting one, and securing the knowledge we need. In similar fashion any lay adult can embark on his or her own adventure in Christian education and quickly discover others who would like to share in it.

THE RAPIDITY OF CHANGE

As we begin to grow in our Christian faith, we can begin to look honestly at what is the most troubling fact of our time: the rapidity of change. This is the underlying cause of much of the unhappiness and despair in our society today. We need to understand and acknowledge that most of us don't really like change. We are always more comfortable with the familiar, with places and people whom we know, and with the comfortable routine with which we grew up. But world-changing science and technology has developed a momentum which will not be stopped. The pace of change is accelerating and will continue to do so. As Christians, we have a special responsibility to look at change in the light of our belief in the God who is in charge of the universe.

Because we are told that God is unchanging, many Christians assume this to mean that we must be unchanging too. But God is God and is unchanging because he is perfect. If we ever hope to grow more nearly up to "the image of God" in which we were made, we have a long way to go! Certainly few of our churches resemble the early Christian congregations about which observers said, "How these Christians love one another." But unfortunately, many lay people who are very ready to accept change in other areas of life object strenuously to any change in the church. It is true that change in the church or the world can be either for the better or for the worse, but the test question is, "Can this be a change which is in the direction of God's will?" It is not an easy question to answer, but it must be tackled.

For example, if relaxing some of the traditional formality of a church service would make strangers or young people feel more welcome, how do we avoid hurting or offending those to whom the old ways are sacred? We, the lay people, *are* the church, or at least 99 percent of it. This is *our* problem, not the minister's. To help people grow into confident, joyful, expectant Christians is one of the primary tasks of the church. And this means that it is your task and mine.

We need to find ways in the church and in our personal and public lives to work on our attitude toward change. As we grow in our understanding of a holy, righteous, and totally loving God and become aware of how far all human institutions fall short of his dreams and hopes, perhaps we will be able to cling less desperately to the past and the familiar and to face with actual hope and anticipation many of the changes we see about us.

There are some interesting themes in the Bible and in theology which relate to change. One of these is the concept of the people of God as a pilgrim people in both the Old and New Testaments. From the time of Abraham through the Book of Revelation, this can be clearly seen. God is always calling people away from the old and the familiar and challenging them to trust and follow him. Abraham, Moses, and the followers of Jesus all found this difficult. Clinging to old securities is a normal human reaction. Yet "By faith Abraham obeyed when he was called to go out . . . and he went out, not knowing where he was to go. . . . For he looked forward to the city which has foundations, whose builder and maker is God" (Heb. 11:8–10). We who believe in and trust God know that the world of today is far from being what a loving God would want, and that we are moving toward a new and very different world. But our task is to free ourselves from any idea that God is imprisoned in the past and be willing to trust that "he who sat upon the throne said, 'Behold, I make all things new' " (Rev. 21:5).

THE COVENANT RELATIONSHIP

Closely allied with this is the Biblical concept of covenant. Both the Old and New Testaments make much of the covenant between God and Israel and between God and his church. And the covenant—the close tie with our Creator—is constantly being renewed. God covenanted with Noah and Abraham and Moses and Jeremiah. And Jesus renewed the covenant at the Last Supper when he said, "This is my blood of the new covenant" (Matt. 26: 28). In our baptism, in the communion service, and every time we commit our lives to Jesus Christ, the covenant is renewed once again. In times of change, we need not become confused and bewildered or lose our sense of purpose. We are bound in a covenant relationship with God and with the people of God (the church). This tells us who we are, why we are here, and what we need to be doing. As a covenant people on a pilgrimage toward a new world, we can have a sense of direction and security which provides hope and courage to dare new things.

If we can begin to grow into confident and daring people as our relationship with God deepens, we will look at the changes taking place in our world as signs of God's activity and will commit ourselves to working for the outcomes we believe God would want. Earlier we looked at two of the major changes of today: the shrinking world and the growing demands of many for freedom and a place in God's world. But there is another factor related to both of these which we need to consider in the light of our faith. This is the growing awareness today of differences, of variety or pluralism. The basis of a great deal of tension, hatred, and strife in the world is our human fear of those who are "different" from us.

To understand what is happening and why we react as we do, we need to remember that through all of human history until our time the majority of people have lived in small groupings—tribes, villages, small towns, or neighborhoods. Usually these were made up of people from similar racial and ethnic origins and of about the same social, economic, and educational level. A person who grows up in such a homogeneous culture cannot avoid assuming that the way "we" do things is the normal and right way. This does not have to be said or taught, it is simply taken for granted. And as long as a person stays isolated from those who behave differently, there is no problem. It is when people begin to travel and encounter different customs and values that trouble brews. If one has always known that mine is the "right" way to behave, the natural reaction is to try—by example, persuasion or force—to change the other person. There is an unspoken assumption that if we are to get along together, we must be alike.

Our question must be, "What does God want?" If God had wanted all human beings to be alike, he could have made us so. Yet we know that God's universe is almost incomprehensibly varied. Not even two flowers or trees are identical, nor are any two human beings exactly alike. Obviously, to the Creator, variety and difference have some profound meaning. Many of us are beginning to sense this meaning as we reach out to those who differ from us. While we know the comfort of being in a group which shares most of the same values and ideas, we soon discover the creativity and stimulation in a group which includes those of different ages, sexes, and backgrounds.

For human beings, differences have often been the root of dislike, persecution, tension, and war. Perhaps the greatest challenge facing the world today, now that we all live in such close contact with one another, is to discover how it is possible to live together peacefully and yet allow for great variety. Can our faith in the God who made us all different help us overcome our almost instinctive feeling that "different" means "wrong"?

RACIAL DIFFERENCES

Think of the problems which racial differences have caused in our own country. In general the white majority has assumed that its customs, values, and life styles were right. When we moved beyond almost total ignoring of racial minorities—black, native American, Hispanic, or Oriental—the general attitude was that if these "different" ones would learn to conform to "our" ways, we would accept them. We even blithely assumed that this was what minority groups wanted! It has taken years of study, discussion, demonstrations, and civil strife to bring us to a point where a few white people understand that minorities do not necessarily want to give up their own values and traditions. The next step, which is just beginning, is for all of us to learn and come to appreciate what the others hold dear. We are beginning to discover that once we really believe a pluralistic society is better than a homogeneous one, we can work together to create it. This will be hard enough in one country. To accomplish it on a world-wide scale is a challenge of the first order.

There are in our own society and in the world other "different" groups who are slowly beginning to sense the positive elements in their difference who can gradually help to enrich life for all of us. These include women in a world where most of the power has been held by men. Young people today, who know so much more than earlier generations of youth, can make great contributions toward building a better future. The handicapped are now militantly demanding that their abilities be recognized. Pluralism is here to stay. It will cause some profound changes in our thinking and action. But if this is God's will, it is good.

As we stretch our concept of pluralism beyond such outward differences as age, sex, and race, we will encounter even more difficult areas such as beliefs and ideologies. Religious differences, which have been at the root of many of the worst persecutions and wars in history, must be the ultimate affront to God. If you and I are committed to trying to do God's will in the world, this is surely the place for us to start. Perhaps we must begin with the premise that God is able—being God—to know, love, and care about every single individual human being. This is so far beyond our comprehension that it is very difficult to grasp. Yet it is an essential part of our belief in the God of the Bible who "numbers the hairs of our heads." In a very deep sense, each individual must make his or her own covenant with God.

Because we are essentially social beings, all religions have taken on a social form—congregations or groups of believers who have shared their experiences and given one another mutual help and strength. But, again, our human tendency to assume that *our* way is the right way has always led groups of believers to try to impose their patterns on others. By the beginning of this century, Christians in the Western world were divided into many different sects and churches. During previous centuries there had been bloody wars fought over religious differences. Toward the end of the last century, God put into the hearts and minds of leaders in different denominations the realization that Christians ought to be actively obeying Jesus' command to "go therefore and make disciples of all nations" (Matt. 28:19).

THE MISSIONARY MOVEMENT

From this grew what has been called the greatest missionary outreach of the Christian church in all of history. Missionaries were sent from this country and from Europe to all parts of Asia, Africa, and the islands of the Pacific. Although it is fashionable now to make fun of these missionaries—to suggest that they were only putting Mother Hubbards on the natives or spreading Western imperialism —this is unfair. They were great and courageous men and women. And their message that God cares even about the poor and oppressed was heard and accepted. Congregations grew and Christianity spread to every part of the globe. God saw to it that his church was planted all around the world just before the invention of the airplane!

Christians in America and Europe were, around 1900, divided into many denominations, and there was little contact between them. But the missionaries quickly discovered that they could not carry out their commission to "win the world for Christ in one generation" if they had to compete with one another. Soon missionaries from many denominations were writing home to say "you must let us work together out here, and you must begin to work together too."

The churches heard them, and in 1910 the first great

ecumenical conference of modern times was convened in Edinburgh—the first International Missionary Conference. For many who came it was a traumatic experience to sit down at a conference table with those from other churches when their forefathers had killed one another over religious differences. But the Conference proved to be a glorious experience. After centuries of rivalry, competition, and isolation, they discovered anew the fact that they all believed in the same God, all read the same Bible, all believed in Jesus Christ, all said the same prayers and psalms, and sang the same hymns. The joy of discovering their unity led to further conferences over the next quarter century. By 1937, representatives of many churches were saying, "It isn't enough to get together in a great world conference every seven or eight years. We need an ongoing structure through which we can work together all the time." And so the idea of a World Council of Churches was born, and it actually came into being in 1948.

Looking back, it seems clear that God knew, as the twentieth century began, that it was to be a time of great upheaval and change. And it is as if God said, "I am going to need my church in all parts of the world." The missionary movement provided this. God also needed to have his church united and working together, and the World Council of Churches met this need. As we look at our tasks as lay Christians living in the global society of today, we should be aware of the world-wide church. Far too many modern Christians know nothing of the church except for the local congregation to which they belong. They think of the church as existing primarily to meet their individual spiritual needs. If we are to venture forth to try to do God's will in the world, we must see ourselves as part of something which begins for us in a local congregation but which ties us to fellow Christians in all parts of the world.

In the fellowship of the World Council of Churches, God seems to be trying out the possibility that under the lordship of Jesus Christ human beings can indeed come together across all the barriers which usually divide us— nation, race, social status, ideology, and even across the broken bonds of Christian churches. In the ecumenical movement of our time, we can begin to learn not how to "do things for" others, but how to work *with* others to solve the terrible problems of our world.

God's hand seems so clear in all this. Take Africa as an example. In the last century God inspired the churches to send missionaries into Africa. Indigenous African culture and religion had been largely destroyed by the colonial powers who then dominated the continent. The missionaries spread the good news of God's love for all human beings and restored to many Africans a sense of their own humanity and dignity. They also provided education for Africans so that when, after the second World War, the African nations began to gain their independence, there were in all of them well-educated and deeply dedicated native church leaders. This group of Christians is one of the great rays of hope in what is today, in some ways, a very dark continent. There is a vigorous All African Council of Churches which brings the Christian leadership of the continent together. And Christianity is growing more rapidly in Africa than anywhere else in the world.

The world of today is a frightening place. Yet there are many signs that God has not abandoned it. As the laity, the great majority of the church, you and I have numerous opportunities today to grow in our understanding of our faith. We also have open to us ways to join hands with Christians in other churches and in all lands to carry out God's will for his entire creation. Were any people ever so fortunate?

Vocation of
the Laity

Findley B. Edge *

3.

... Into the World, So Send I You

THE CONCEPT OF THE MINISTRY OF THE laity has had a resurgence during the last few decades. Perhaps it had its beginnings in the underground church in Europe during the second World War. After the war the emergence of the Evangelical Lay Academies, particularly in Germany, gave a strong impetus to this emphasis with their programs designed to bridge the gap between the church and the world by seeking to relate the gospel to vocations and social structures. In the United States, Sam Shoemaker led laymen to share their faith in such a way they became "priests to each other" as well as in the world. Elton Trueblood has also been a strong influence in this area. And in 1958 the publication of the book, *A Theology of the Laity,* by Hendrik Kraemer, struck a responsive chord in many people.

This seemed to be "an idea whose time had come." But unfortunately the response by the laity has not been as great as we might have expected. While we cannot say

. . * DR. FINDLEY B. EDGE is professor of religious education at Southern Baptist Theological Seminary, Louisville, Kentucky. He is the author of *The Greening of the Church* (Word).

there has been no response or progress in this area, yet when the total picture is viewed both among Protestants and Catholics, the relative progress has been small indeed.

Still the ministry of the laity is one of the "in" topics for our time. Indeed its very popularity poses a real problem. The ministry of the laity has had so many good books and articles written about it and so many sermons and addresses delivered that we are in danger of drowning the concept in an ocean of words before the reality is ever born. This is not to say that more explanation and deeper understanding are not needed, but it is to say that the time for "mere words" is past. The time for action and implementation is here.

THE NEED FOR UNDERSTANDING AND MOTIVATION

This is easier said than done. Serious and difficult problems are immediately confronted. First, there is the problem related to understanding. In spite of all that has been spoken and written about this Biblical teaching, the large majority of church members really have no serious understanding that they have been called by God to be the basic ministers. Or, if they do have some understanding that they are ministers, they have either a mistaken or a limited idea as to where and how this ministry is to be expressed. A second major problem relates to motivation. A large segment of Christians have neither the desire nor the willingness in any serious way to seek to be ministers for God in the world. These people are willing to attend an occasional morning worship service, but trying to be a "minister" through one's vocation is simply taking religion much too far.

But assuming one understands he is a minister, and assuming one is sufficiently committed as a Christian so that he is willing to be a minister, there is still a question of major importance that has to be answered: "In the complex and hard-nosed world in which I live and work, what is it I am to do to be a minister? I do not want to give the impression in my vocation that I am a 'holy Joe' nor do I want to stick out like a 'sore thumb.' What are the opportunities that I may now be overlooking? How do I express this ministry in concrete terms? Be practical and specific." It is to these questions we now turn our attention.

The layman spends most of his waking hours in his vocation or related to some structure of society. What are some ways he might express his ministry as a Christian in this so-called secular area? There are so many vocations and the decisions and situations which laymen constantly face are so complex that each person must make his own decision as to "how" his ministry is to be expressed. However, in an attempt to give the layman some guidance, examples of what certain people have done in specific situations in an effort to express their Christian ministry will be given. Perhaps this will stimulate us to discover ways we can express our ministry in our situation through our vocation or some structure of society.

Increasingly we find that being honest is no longer a "simple" matter. Our newspapers report practices that are highly questionable in terms of basic honesty. In business and in government questions have been raised about "gifts" to individuals purportedly from foreign interests seeking to influence decisions that would be favorable to their special interests. And in business there has been evidence of multinational corporations giving large sums of money to foreign officials to secure contracts for their companies.

Perhaps, then, the place to begin our consideration of "how" is in the area of basic honesty. The president of a small chain of apothecaries tells of an experience he had with a wholesale pharmaceutical company. Over the years, ordering as much as he did, inevitably there were errors in shipment. Sometimes the error was in overshipment. If he ordered one box of an item, they might send a dozen, or if he ordered ten boxes they might send twenty. When this happened, he always wrote a letter explaining what had happened and quite often he simply kept the extra and sent a check to cover the charges. One day a salesman came in accompanied by a second person who introduced himself as the vice president of the wholesale pharmaceutical company. He had come, he said, to meet the head of a company that did business like that. It had been his experience, he said, that when the error was in the wholesale company's favor, he always heard from the retail apothecary. But when the error was in the apothecary's favor, he rarely heard from them.

A similar situation happened to a young and struggling oil shipping company in the south. A major petroleum company contracted with this small shipping company for a rather large job. In writing up the contract the petroleum company made a mistake amounting to a large sum of money. Without even considering what such a "windfall" could do for a struggling shipping company, the owner immediately contacted the petroleum company and called their attention to the mistake. This experience had a happy ending. The official in the petroleum company was so impressed with the honesty and integrity of such a person that he gave the man more and more business. He also shared this experience with friends in other petroleum companies so that soon the small shipping company had more business than it could handle.

GOD DOES NOT PROMISE US "A ROSE GARDEN"

However, not all Christian actions or decisions have a "happy ending." There are times when the contract will be lost, when the business fails, when the Christian decision leads to suffering. God does not promise us "a rose garden." For example, in the area of honesty some fundamental and difficult questions are raised. An advertising firm is approached by one of its largest clients to develop an advertising campaign for a pharmaceutical product which has no demonstrated therapeutic value supportable by scientific evidence. A vice president of the advertising firm calls in a junior officer and tells him to work up an advertising campaign that will be acceptable to the client. The junior officer inquires, "What will this item do?" The vice president replies, "Nothing! That's not your responsibility! You just work up a campaign that will sell the stuff!" How does a Christian react in that situation? Of course the question must also be raised about the honesty of a pharmaceutical company which will market a product for which there is no scientific support for its therapeutic value.

This raises the question of how a Christian might respond in a situation where there is a serious conflict between his Christian convictions and a requirement placed upon him by his company. One person may decide that his ministry is to stay within the company and seek to be a change agent. However, there may come times, after one has tried all other options, when a Christian, on the basis of his convictions and commitment to Christ, will have to resign because he cannot be a part of carrying out policies that have been decided.

The president of a large corporation had to make such a decision. His company was bought by one of the massive conglomerates, and new policies for the operation of the company were passed down to him. He said, "As president of the company I was asked to 'allow certain things to happen' that I did not think were proper. This was not doing anything illegal, but just doing some things I thought did not reflect Christian principles. Not only that, I didn't think these things were morally right. So I had to make a decision. I prayed and asked God to help me make that decision. Of course I also talked the matter over with my family because they were integrally involved. I sought the counsel of friends whose opinions I valued. I finally made the decision to leave the company. This is not easy to do when one's salary is in the six figure category. But there are times in big business when one is asked to compromise one's ethics and Christian convictions. It is in such times one has to decide, 'Who are you?' Or more specifically one has to decide, 'Whose are you?' One has to decide whether he is going to follow unethical principles or follow the Christian principles to which he has committed his life."

CHRISTIANITY AND BUSINESS

However, most businessmen who are also seriously committed Christians are convinced that there is no necessary conflict between running a successful business and following Christian principles. The top executive of a corporation listed on the New York Stock Exchange said big business does not have to be a profit-centered, money-grabbing kind of profession. One can adopt Christian principles and still be successful. Obviously the concept of profit does have to be taken into account. Profit is a return on capital investment. A proper return on investment is necessary to replenish one's economic base for growth. But unlimited profit does not have to be a company's major, and certainly not sole, objective. One must be concerned about his employees and their welfare. He must be concerned about the product he produces. There are some who cut corners and make inferior products to get more profits. Obviously, this is not right, and it certainly is not Christian. Being a Christian in business adds a sense of responsibility to one's life. It is the concept of trusteeship—spiritual trusteeship. Stewardship is a part of the Christian's total life.

The president of a company in Texas was asked to cite an example of what he did beyond being honest in his business dealings and making a good product to express his ministry as a Christian. In responding he cited the fact that the year before he was invited to become president of the corporation he now heads, the company had lost several million dollars. He was employed to come in and "turn the company around." Soon after he arrived he decided to have a staff retreat—a type of organizational meeting—for the top executive leadership in the company. As a basis for this retreat he used the material in 1 Corinthians 12 where Paul speaks of the church having many parts but one body. Each part is important and necessary. Each part has its own function and fits properly into its own place. "I told the group," he said, "this is the basis on which we are going to operate this business. We are going to be a family. We are going to be a genuinely caring fellowship."

The president of the company concluded by saying, "We have earnestly sought to carry out this family concept. If one of the officers or other workers is having marital difficulties, we have tried to build relationships that say to him, 'We really care what is happening to you in every aspect of your life. And if you believe us we want you to feel free to share this hurt in your life with someone or some group in the company you feel you can trust.' Or if someone is having serious illness in the family, or if someone is having difficulty with a teenage child, whatever the situation, we want him to find an individual or group with whom he feels free to open up the deeper parts of his life. As president I try to set the example. I have a group with whom I share my life and with whom I pray." Then he said, "It just so happens that this is not only good Christianity, it is also good business. Within three months after the retreat, the company was in the black." Then as a concluding statement he said, "I am convinced that the New Testament is the best business organizational manual ever written."

In the economic structures there are subtle—but legitimate—ways multinational corporations can receive special benefits because they have sufficient power and resources to influence the "rules" by which the "game is played." For example, a company that sells a major product in the United States such as an automobile, a large appliance, farm machinery, or something similar may have a subsidiary company in a developing nation like Argentina that makes parts for the product. This subsidiary sells the parts at a very low price to another subsidiary in another country, like Panama. Minor things may be done to the parts

in Panama and then they are sold to the company in the
United States for a very high price, practically the same
price for which the part is sold in the United States. Thus
minimal profits are made in Argentina and the United
States and minimal taxes are paid in each of these countries. The corporation, through its subsidiary, has made its
major profit in Panama, but Panama does not tax profits.
Such a practice is certainly legitimate but what about the
ethics involved in the responsibility of the corporation both
to Argentina and the United States?

An extremely positive and hopeful sign is the growing
evidence that multinational corporations are becoming
more sensitive and responsive to the "human factors" as
well as having a natural concern for profits in their total
operation.

ETHICS IN BIG BUSINESS

A multinational company with headquarters in Indiana
has on its staff in an executive position a former professor
of ethics at Yale whose task it is to help the corporation be
sensitive to the social, moral, and ethical issues involved
in the complex relationships the corporation has to its
stockholders, its employees, the community in which it is
located, the country in which it is located, and the governments to which it is related. At present he is the "only one
of his kind." However, he says he does not believe this is
merely a "fad" due to the ethical examination the United
States is going through at this time. He sees signs of a
similar trend in other corporations in this country and
around the world.

The leaders of this corporation see such an approach to
business to be an expression of a deep religious commitment. But they also recognize that such an approach in
reality is simply "corporate self-interest." While many
corporations are still debating whether or not a company
has a social responsibility to the country in which it is

located, this corporation is convinced that to be concerned about the total conditions of the country in which
it is located and to be concerned about the basic needs of
the people in terms of food, shelter, health, and safety is
not only morally right, it is also good business.

How does this emphasis work out in practical action?
The basic principle on which the company operates is:
before the company will act, it must be fully determined
that what is in the best interest of the company is also in
the best interest of the public. Two examples will illustrate
this principle. Recently a tax measure was being considered
by Congress. When this tax proposal was studied consci-
entiously and objectively by the staff related to ethical concerns, it was decided that this tax probably was in the best
interest of the public. But it was certainly not in the best
interest of the corporation. In fact, the corporation would
be "stung" by the tax. However, the corporation did not
lobby against the tax. The company did not "act" because
the interest of the corporation and the public did not
coincide. In this instance, not to act was in fact a positive
action.

As another example, the Congress was considering the
Clean Air Act. "What we did was to step back and try to
figure out what the optimal strategy would be from a public interest viewpoint, a strategy that would reconcile the
various competing claims from an ethical, a value-based
perspective. How do you balance the advantages of technology against environmental damage and health hazards
(both proven damage and hazards that our evolving knowledge might turn up)? Down the line, what are the desirable
trade-offs between energy and mobility on the one hand
and emission controls on the other? It's an issue that goes
to the heart of our business. We make engines. . . . We
came up with a suggested regulatory strategy that we
felt touched all the legitimate bases, and we provided
technical data from which such a legislative strategy could
be developed." * In this instance the corporation acted

vigorously, positively, and constructively because the best interest of the public and the best interest of the corporation did coincide.

Several years ago the Council on Religion and International Affairs along with other philanthropic and nonprofit institutions "began to study its portfolio, which contains securities of international corporations, from a moral perspective. Discussions attending its social investment concerns resulted in the conviction that CRIA should and could further the important and difficult discussion on the ethics of investment by organizing a seminar. Out of this first seminar came the book *People/Profits: The Ethics of Investment.* The current volume is the result of a second such seminar. These two seminars in turn have helped CRIA to embark on a full-scale Corporate Consultation Program, which concerns itself with the social responsibility of multinational corporations." [1] These two studies point up the enormous complexity of the ethical issues faced by multinational corporations, but they also indicate a growing awareness by these corporations of human and social values as well as profit.

In the structures of government a lawyer used his vocational expertise to minister in a very positive way. After telling of a deeply moving Christian experience, he said, "My business life, too, has changed radically. . . . My interest now is helping people to solve their problems, whereas before I would think about my fee and not care about my client's personal needs.

"A very gratifying result of my change in attitude and interest was to see the enactment of legislation . . . that will allow judges in Texas to require people in Texas to obtain professional counseling during divorce proceedings.

"My part in helping to get this new law on the books consisted of some rather extensive research, which I presented to our local bar association, which in turn presented it to the state bar. As a result, I was appointed to the State Bar Committee, and with the help of a law professor at

Baylor University, I drafted the legislation which was finally enacted as an amendment to our Texas 'family code.'

"What excites me in a divorce case is to have a client ask, in one way or another, 'What is the purpose of my life? I've done all I know to do, and everything has gone wrong.' Almost invariably I find that such a person has failed to make use of the resources of Christian faith." [2]

CHRISTIANITY IN POLITICS

In spite of the critical attacks that have been made on national government and the consequent low esteem into which it has fallen in the minds of many, there are a number of committed Christians in national politics who are serious in their attempt to render a Christian ministry in this structure of our society. One example is Congressman John Anderson of Illinois who is now chairman of the House Republican Conference. ". . . it is said that he could have succeeded Gerald Ford in the important post of Minority Leader of the House if party leaders could have trusted him to vote their way all the time. Instead, say observers, Anderson has a reputation of voting his conscience on sensitive issues. ('If I had that kind of record as a congressman,' commented a *Time* reporter privately, 'I'd want it engraved on my tombstone.')

" 'I've been ridiculed by some Republican colleagues for acting on my feelings of moral conscience rather than for political advantage,' Anderson acknowledges. 'They think I'm pointing my finger at them and saying they have less conscience. I don't want to be self-righteous, but on the other hand, I don't want to become so lacking in resolve that I succumb to that kind of pressure. I think the most important thing I can do is show that I'm willing to follow the dictates of a Christian conscience, even at the expense of losing office.' Anderson was one of the successful survivors in '74.

"Anderson has put his political future on the line more

than once by voting against the wishes of many constituents.
For example, he cast the deciding vote in the Rules Committee for an Open Housing bill on the eve of Dr. Martin
Luther King's funeral. Two years earlier he had voted
against open housing. He says his decision to switch came
through prayer and meditation on a Bible passage: 'For if
a man is in Christ he becomes a new person altogether
. . . All this is God's doing, for he has reconciled us to
himself through Jesus Christ; and he has made us agents
of the reconciliation.' " [3]

Undoubtedly the most visible Christian in national politics is President Jimmy Carter. Mary McGrory, a national
syndicated columnist, wrote recently of an encounter she
had with two young men in Italy. "They wanted to talk
about Jimmy Carter.

" 'He is molto bravo,' said the one with the mustache.
'He is open, he is honest,' he went on. 'He is a nuclear
scientist, and engineer. For us in Italy, this is very important. We must have nuclear power. We import 90 percent of our energy, and we can't afford it.'

" 'He is religious,' said the one with the blue velvet
jacket.

"Is that important in a country, where, according to the
figures, only 50 percent (of the Catholics) actually practice their religion?

" 'Yes,' he replied. Most people run to the church and
confess their sins, then they go out and do them all over
again. Carter is really religious.' " [4]

Irrespective of one's religious or political persuasion,
everyone knows that Jimmy Carter is "really religious"
and in the complex and ambiguous arena of world politics
this fact had come through with such authenticity it impressed at least these two young men and it was felt to be
so sufficiently significant a national columnist wrote a col-
umn about it. This is expressing a Christian ministry
through one's vocation.

Not only does the layman have the opportunity to express

his Christian ministry to large groups of people, he also has the opportunity through his vocation to minister to individuals. The top executive of a multinational motel chain is a deeply committed Christian. In an effort to express his Christian concern for persons, he caused his motel chain to become the first to employ a full-time chaplain. Now the chain has more than 1,700 chaplains on call. They report that in ten years they have had 100,000 callers and have probably prevented 3,000 suicides.[5]

Again, a number of questions arise. How extensively should a Christian business man share his personal concepts with his employees or friends? How much, if any, should he utilize the resources of his company to further Christian causes? Is it right to utilize the resources of others to further a specific belief a top executive may have? The president of one corporation answered these questions in this way: "I solved these questions for myself in a rather simple way. I accepted myself as I was and I accepted others as they were, always wanting for them the relationship Christ offered and the deeper experience for those who were already Christian. I do not have the right to utilize resources of the company for personal Christian projects. However, when our company built a twelve-story office building, on my recommendation and with the approval of the Board of Directors, we built a chapel as a part of the building. This was not a 'Christian' chapel. It was a meditation room where people of any faith could go for meditation. But including it was a small way in which I could say that spiritual matters were important to me.

"Also I do not believe I have the right to impose my religious beliefs on the employees or anyone else. Nor do I feel a compulsion to 'witness' to every person who comes into my office. Yet, I do have a Bible on my desk which in itself is a witness. On the other hand, I try very hard to be sensitive to opportunities to give a witness when such seems appropriate (and these are far more numerous than we generally think). A secretary in the company indicated that she had decided to quit her job. She came to say good-by which is a sort of custom in our company. In the conversation she indicated she was quitting to travel with her son. I told her how nice it was that she would have this opportunity. When I said that, she seemed to 'cloud up' and tears came to her eyes. Then under great emotion she said the real reason she was quitting her job was she was running away from a homosexual husband. I continued to talk with her for a while and finally she said she was really disgusted with life because she had found no meaning for her existence. I reached in the drawer of my desk and got some material I keep there related to Christ and the meaning He gives to life. We talked a while longer and then I had prayer with her. Later she called back on the phone, full of joy now, and told me she had accepted Christ as the Lord of her life." Too many laymen, instead of ministering to the lady, would have tried to comfort her and usher her out of the office.

CHRISTIANITY AND THE MEDICINE PROFESSION

Physicians, because they often meet people in crisis periods of life, have a unique opportunity to express a specifically Christian ministry. Geoffrey Kitson, a layman and formerly a Commander in the British Royal Navy and now President of Faith At Work, shared recently an encounter he and his family had with Dr. Wilder Penfield, the world-famous neurosurgeon. Mr. Kitson said that his son had terrible epileptic seizures due to an injury at birth. The problem was so severe it could not be controlled through medication. Through the years they went to numerous doctors and every one of them refused to operate because they could not be sure where the damage was located and thus could not be sure where the incision should be made. Finally they heard of Dr. Penfield and went to him for consultation. After a thorough examination of the boy,

Dr. Penfield indicated he would be glad to operate. Mr. Kitson said the operation took eleven and one-half hours. During the operation a resident doctor came out to give a "progress report" and said, "I have never seen a man operate with more steady hands!" After the operation (which turned out to be a complete success), when Dr. Penfield came to give the report to the family, Mr. Kitson tried to express to him the thanks and gratitude of the entire family. Dr. Penfield quietly replied, "Don't thank me. There is One greater than I who guides my hand." This was a brief but a powerful Christian witness.

Doctors also face the reality of death and the agony that attends this experience. A pediatrician was attending a young girl who was hopelessly ill. He said, "I knew all I could do was to try to 'be with' the family. They had two other children. So I made it a point to be present at the end. When the child expired, I asked the family if I could have prayer with them. They responded positively and we did. Several months later, at Christmas, I received an eight page letter from the mother. She said out of the tragedy of her child's death God had become a much deeper reality. And now she is a 'priest' for others. She has a ministry to parents whose children are facing death."

A physician, who taught part-time at a university medical school, shared an experience he had with a young person on drugs. "One day," he said, "the chairman of medicine called and asked if I would talk to a neighbor who had a son on drugs. We had a man in the department who was a specialist in the area of drugs, and I wondered why he didn't ask this doctor. However, an appointment was made for the father and the boy. Later they called and broke the appointment. For some reason I prayed for them all weekend. I didn't know much about the problem or about the family, but what I knew scared me to death. I knew the father was a graduate of the Harvard School of Economics and undoubtedly was much smarter than I was. Another appointment was made and this time they came.

"The father explained the situation as he saw it and the son did the same. As I listened I felt they were both right in their analysis but they were at a stalemate in communicating with each other. I listened to them about an hour and said if they would like to talk again, I would be happy to see them. Then I said to them, 'I perceive that your problem is a spiritual problem.' I had no notion how that would be received, but all of a sudden the father became very warm. So that encouraged me to reach up on my shelf and give them a book to read. I didn't hear from them again. About three or four months later a fellow and I were at church and he asked what I had done to _____, and he mentioned the boy's name. I didn't know how to respond because I didn't want to reveal any confidential information about the family, so I asked him, why? He said the boy had been asking all kinds of questions about the Bible. He had completely straightened up from his drug problem. It turned out that after reading that book he became a Christian, and he has remained steadfast in his Christian commitment for over four years. But, of course, I took a risk in this situation. . . . I felt a particular leading in this instance, and it turned out to be right. But I really was vulnerable."

Another type of ministry that is becoming increasingly widespread is one in which a group of people get together enough capital to purchase an old and dilapidated apartment building. They refurbish the apartments, generally doing most of the work themselves, and rent the apartments back to the same people who had them at the same price they were paying before the cleanup. A group of businessmen got together and did this in New York City on a relatively large scale. Churches are also engaging in this type of ministry. The Church of the Saviour in Washington, D.C. may have been the first of any group to render this type of service. The Church of the Covenant in Louisville, Kentucky, is also engaged in this ministry. There is one of these projects in Richmond, Virginia, that is black owned and black operated. Several of those involved do so as a Christian ministry. The American Baptist Convention has had such success in supervising this type of project that groups are now coming to them for special training.

A layman in Georgia who works for an oil company began to speculate in land a few years ago. His speculation proved profitable, and soon he owned considerable real estate. About this time, in a conference held in his church, he felt that God was "calling" him to minister to young people who were trying to "kick" the drug habit. After considerable personal struggle, he became convinced that the Lord wanted him to take his best piece of property in North Georgia and develop a type of half-way house for these young people where they could come and live for several months or longer, where they could work and help grow their own food, and where they would be related to Christian companionship and teaching. He and his wife organized a nonprofit corporation and set about the task of raising the funds for this undertaking. Now the center is in operation and has a full-time director. One man and one woman can make a difference.

The individual who is seriously involved in seeking to express his ministry needs a support system to assist him in and to hold him accountable for fulfilling this ministry. This support system should be provided by the church and should be specific and practical.

1. *Educational Support.* This support in general terms will come from a variety of sources. For example, spiritual support will come through the inspiration and guidance the person receives from the worship services. It will also come from a consistent and meaningful devotional life. But there needs to be support that is more specifically and directly related to the layman's expression of ministry in the world. For example, he needs to be provided with Bible study in which he is led to grapple with and to seek to understand the teachings of Holy Scripture and the demands these teachings lay upon all of God's people as they

try to express in concrete ways these teachings in our kind
of world. As the other side of this coin, the layman also
needs to be led in a correspondingly serious study of the
general ethical issues we are facing in the world and the
specific ethical issues one tends to face in his vocation and
influence. The issues laymen face daily are so complex and
ambiguous, the principles involved are often so contradictory, that no serious or intelligent Christian response
can be made without a deep awareness of the meaning of
the total gospel and a careful exploration of the factors
involved in the particular issue. The church should provide
this guidance.

In addition the church should also provide support by
seeking to help the layman discern his gift(s), discover his
"call," and experience the affirmation of a commissioning
service.[6] One reason the layman often fails to get involved
in ministry for God is that he thinks he has nothing to offer. Unfortunately, the emphasis and approach in some
religious groups has tended to give their members a very
low image of themselves. Their attitude is, "I'm nobody.
I don't have any talents. I can't do anything." (This is supposed to reflect their humility and their lack of pride.)
They seemingly do not understand that such an attitude
borders on blasphemy. Christians are gifted people! God
has given his people these gifts because he wanted them to
utilize them in ministry for him in the world.

In this connection, there are three weaknesses in the life
of the church today that need to be rectified immediately.
First, with the strong emphasis the Bible places on the gifts
God has given his people for the work of ministering, the
church has failed to give anything like an adequate emphasis to this teaching. This must be changed. Second, with
the variety of organizations and meetings churches have,
there is almost no organization nor meeting which is specifically designed to help the layman discover his gifts.
This needs to be changed. Third, there is little material
available today designed to give guidance to the church in

knowing how to help the layman discover his gifts. The fact is we know little about this tremendously important area. This needs to be changed.

It is my opinion that God also "calls" laymen to certain ministries. Every layman is to be a minister through his vocation and through those structures of society to which he is related in his daily existence. But, in addition to this, there are also times when God calls a layman to a particular ministry. This special ministry might be related to some aspect of the institutional church or it may be related to some needy area of society. One's gift(s) gives a hint as to what this ministry might be—what in the world and where in the world—because one's "call" is always related to one's gift(s). It would be a great support for a layman if a group to which he was intimately related were to say, "We affirm this gift in you and we also affirm, on the basis of what you have shared with us and what we have shared with you over the past months, that God is calling you to this particular expression of ministry in his vineyard and we will support you in it."

In addition, it would be a great source of support if the group or, preferably, the entire church were to have a commissioning service for the individual (or for the group if the entire group is involved in the same ministry). A layman said, "My church ought to commission me as president of my corporation." Or, a group who feels called to minister to adult illiterates should be commissioned to this ministry by the church. A liturgy ought to be prepared in which pastor, congregation, and group (or individual) would respond to God and to each other in terms of "call" and commitment to this particular ministry. Not only would such a service be a great support to the individual(s) involved, it would also mean that the church would not "load" the person with other responsibilities so he would have both the time and the freedom to fulfill this ministry.

Commissioning also presupposes that one must be trained. This means the layman has taken his ministry so seriously that he has secured the training necessary to fulfill it. Commissioning also means the church assumes responsibility for holding the layman accountable for this ministry. Therefore, there ought to be times, formal and informal, for "check-in," for reporting on how things are going. A person may be having an extremely difficult time in a given area and may need the prayer support of the entire church. Or a person may have become lax or busy with other things and the Christian community may need to have an accounting with reference to the area the layman stated was his call and ministry. To hold a person accountable is an expression of love for him. This says you care. To ignore him is an expression of nonlove. Or a person may have had a particularly positive experience in which God manifested himself in an unusual way, and this joy needs to be shared with the community.

2. *Group Support.* In addition to the educational support, the Christian involved in ministry will find support in the form of a small group that meets weekly (or at least periodically) to share their lives and their struggles and to pray together. This is not an "introvert" group concerned only about the inner life of those present. The inner life is a concern, of course. However, in this group the eyes of the participants are turned outward—to the world. Their major concerns are with the issues and the concerns with which they are struggling and the people to whom they are seeking to minister. This is a group "on mission" with God.

Sometimes the group may be composed of people from the same congregation or it may be made up of people from a variety of churches, both Catholic and Protestant. In such a group the individual often will find a more personal approach to the support he needs.

The president of a corporation told of his experience with such a group. He said the presidents of twelve businesses in a large southern city meet together monthly just for the purpose of sharing with each other on a spiritual basis. Just because a person is in the top echelon of leadership in business does not mean he doesn't need spiritual guidance and spiritual support. It may mean he needs it more. These persons may also be members of the board of directors of a bank, members of the Chamber of Commerce, members of a wide variety of community institutions. They are concerned about economic needs, social needs, housing needs—every kind of need in the community. Certainly, my friend said, we share our own personal spiritual concerns, but we also share concerns in our vocation and other areas in which we are involved.

"We ask, 'Where are you today? What are your needs? Where is it hurting for you? What can we pray with you about?' The mayor of the city may be there in the group. We say, 'Mr. Mayor (of course we use his first name), what's going on in your life? We see by the newspaper you are facing some difficult problems. Can we pray with you about them?' After this group gets together to share, to discuss, to pray, they then go into the various sectors of society to make decisions. But they go with the spiritual support and guidance of this group and the decisions they make in the secular sector will be influenced by this spiritual experience." The person, knowing he has the care and support of this kind of group, is much more likely to dare to make decisions or take courses of action based on Christian convictions rather than succumb to pressures of profits, expediency, or special interest groups.

A principle in the doctrine of incarnation may also be operable here. God uniquely revealed himself in the Person of his Son. Today he continues to reveal himself to us through persons. Through the ministry of people in such a support group, God in the Person of the Holy Spirit may become real to us in a special way so that a power beyond our own is released within us to enable us to fulfill the ministry in the world to which he has called us.

NOTES

* Published in *Quest*.

1. Richard A. Jackson, (Editor), *The Multinational Corporation and Social Policy* (Special Reference to General Motors in South Africa). New York: Praeger Publishers, 1974, p. v.

2. Ted M. Anderson, "Can a Man Change?" *Faith At Work* (June 1970), pp. 4–5.

3. James C. Hefley and Edward E. Plowman, *Washington: Christians in the Corridors of Power.* Wheaton: Tyndale House, 1975, p. 119.

4. Mary McGrory, "Jimmy Carter is 'new man' in the Old World." *The Louisville Times,* Friday, June 10, 1977, p. A6.

5. Kemmons Wilson, "A Place to Worship," *Saturday Evening Post,* April, 1977, p. 37.

6. For a more detailed discussion of the areas of gift, call, and commissioning, see Edge, Findley, B., *The Greening of the Church.* Waco: Word Books, 1971, pp. 135–175.

Joseph Cunneen *

4.

Toward a Faith of Our Own

God has no grandchildren! each gen-
eration, each individual has to make his/her own decision
for Christ. Most of my students have attended Roman
Catholic or Protestant churches when they were younger,
and a large majority have gone to parochial schools or
Sunday schools or through some other religious education
program. What concerns me is not so much the low level
of basic information about Christianity that they have
gained from their studies but that, once genuine discussion
gets started, I invariably encounter a common complaint,
"We were never asked before to make religion something
that is *ours*."

Christianity, one quickly discovers, means church, which
they aren't very much against but think of as something that
priests and ministers do. My students know, of course,
that many others, often including their own mothers and

---

* Joseph Cunneen is editor of *Cross Currents*, A Journal of
Roman Catholic Opinion, West Nyack, New York. He is also a
professor at Mercy College, Dobbs Ferry, N.Y. He has written
for such journals as *Thought, Commonweal, Midstream, Christianity*, and *Crisis, Esprit*, and *The Nation*.

fathers, go to church but apparently believe they remain completely passive there while something is done for them by people who are officially "religious."

A PRIESTLY MONOPOLY?

Some may think I am exaggerating or that my experience is only the product of a special situation, but I am convinced that attitudes not so different from these are widely shared, even by regular churchgoers. The sad result is that despite the strong New Testament protest against a priestly monopoly of religion, a powerful set of assumptions have become widely diffused which have encouraged too many of us to practice our Christianity as if it were a religion of the clergy.

There are, of course, historical reasons for our situation. Within Roman Catholicism, for example, the defensive reaction to the Reformation emphasis on the common priesthood of the faithful has still not been completely overcome. But none of us should use the clerical overemphasis that exists in the various (including Protestant) ecclesiastical structures of present-day Christianity as an alibi for ignoring the invitation of Christ to be his disciples in our offices and factories, in our homes and neighborhoods. If we are to accept the implicit challenge of my students and begin to internalize our faith, we must deepen our awareness that we—the laity—are the Church already present in the world.

The latter is no fancy phrase for an inspirational pep talk but a sobering reminder of an opportunity and a challenge. The Redemption has already taken place; there remains the labor of "restoring all things in Christ." This means beginning from where we are, in the real circumstances of our lives, with a sharpened sense of our talents and limitations. Each of us has been given a task: to organize this course, to prepare this meal, to assemble these parts, to deliver these products. It might be more peaceful in church, it might be more edifying to hear the organ and look at stained-glass windows, but our worship of God will most frequently be expressed in one or a combination of these routine secular occupations.

It is instructive to observe how my students, often quite outspoken in their criticisms of the churches and of church-goers, quickly become tongue-tied when asked how we together could make a given course or their overall school experience a closer embodiment of their own highest values. Some will jump to misinterpret my questions as a desire to institute some kind of required group prayer; one Catholic student from a parochial school background illustrated their general confusion by complaining that, since ours is a secular college, it would be inappropriate to put up a crucifix in the classroom! Even those alert to the imper-sonality of the educational process are wary of sharing responsibility for determining its day-to-day practice. It is easier to go on blaming faculty and administration than to take an inventory of student needs, accept joint assign-ments in class, gather information regarding the college's nonfaculty employees, help me revise the curriculum for the course they have just endured, or even simply to study together and support one another.

A SENSE OF POWERLESSNESS

My students are hardly to blame for their sense of power-lessness; most of them are so victimized by the all-pervasive pressures of the American competitive ethos that they find it difficult to conceive of learning as involving anything more than the acquisition of quickly negotiable bits of unrelated information. Nevertheless, the sadly ironic result is that the passivity they criticize when discussing Chris-tianity or religion is the underlying pattern of their student careers. There is much of the same split between the edu-cational process and what my students have made "their own" as there is between routine Sunday churchgoing and

what we lay people actually express in the way we do our
jobs the rest of the week. In varying degrees, both are
products of a truncated Christian teaching in which salvation is presented in exclusively individualistic terms and the
demands of morality are limited to the private sphere, with
special emphasis on sex.

How else can we account for the brutal fact that despite
the impressive statistical sense in which the United States
can still be thought of as a "Christian country," there are so
few signs of a meaningful Christian presence in our institutions and our culture? Decisions which intimately
affect the lives of our children, determine the use of natural
resources for decades to come, and possibly lead to the
destruction of life on our planet are made as if Christianity
had nothing to say, as if Christians were not present in our
board rooms, at our conference tables, or in Washington,
D.C. Unless we are to be satisfied by such cosmetic touches
as the presence of a minister and/or priest at presidential
inaugurations or by righteous denunciations of others—
politicians, corporation executives, and nonbelievers seem
to be the favorite targets for this kind of sermonizing—
there is no way to avoid our own share of responsibility
and to look more closely at the way in which we perform
our particular tasks and the relation of these small efforts
to a world in travail.

SOME PROBING QUESTIONS

Although most of us will hardly need to be told to do an
honest day's work, it is still easy for us to forget that how
we perform our tasks does make a significant difference.
To think otherwise, it seems to me, is to make light of the
reality of the Incarnation. What we used to call "women's
work" provides a clue to a corrected attitude: how would
we respond to a mother who said that she was willing to
prepare her family's meals for fifty weeks during the year
to make it possible for her to have two weeks at the sea-

shore in the summer? Without ignoring the fact that so many jobs are boring and repetitive, we must still remember to respect the materials we are working with; we are at the service of the work to be done. Could it be done more skillfully? Are there ways in which the enterprise which our work supports could be made more human, more caring? Again, does it matter that a Christian is doing the work?

These may seem naive questions, but their intention is not to solicit pious answers. My disposition is not improved by being told that my tailor goes to Mass every day if the trousers he returns to me still don't fit. Good intentions rightly become suspect when not supported by thorough professionalism. But if being a good worker is, in a sense, the foundation-stone of the layman's understanding of vocation, it should quickly become apparent that each of us also has the responsibility of recognizing that our skills may serve a variety of purposes. The same complex equation by which a surgeon might make sure that his genius is not available exclusively for the well-to-do may also be used by the secretary in a company that practices racial discrimination, by the banker in a firm with investments and loans in repressive foreign regimes, or by the contractor for a builder who uses shoddy materials—and by all of us as citizens and consumers.

With unemployment in many ways our society's equivalent to excommunication, let us be wary of any holier-than-thou attitude about the jobs people take to pay for basic necessities. But many of us have wider areas of choice— have a voice in company policy or can affect a decision on a significant capital investment. What criteria are we to employ? We know we cannot find explicit answers in Scripture, recent social encyclicals of the popes, or declarations of the World Council of Churches. But unless we are penetrated by their spirit how will we resist the strong pressures to look only at "the bottom line" of profitability? The American economy is mostly controlled by men who

consider themselves Christians; it would be naive to assume
that they are any more wicked than the rest of us, or that
many of them are deliberately offering goods and services
which they believe are worthless. Yet we also realize that
this is not enough to guarantee that the resources, the
wealth, and the labor of our great country are genuinely
in the service of the common good. What makes it possible
to go on building resort hotels and suburban middle class
developments while ignoring the housing needs of our
inner-city poor is not the malice of a few individuals but
the weight of our whole economic structure, supported by
unexamined assumptions as to what stewardship means.

SUPPORT GROUPS

The modest successes of contemporary lay movements
within Roman Catholicism have all developed out of an
understanding of an apostolate of like to like. Once it is
understood that the world we are called upon to transform
will not be significantly affected by individual piety, more
and more Christians should see the value of joining with
others in small, perhaps quite informal, support groups to
examine our working or professional lives in their many-
faceted implications. Just as many of my students tell me
that they drifted into a particular course or a given major
because they felt powerless, or are forced to cheat on exams
because "everybody does it," lawyers, nurses, executives,
and workers on the assembly line need to feel they are not
alone in confronting "the system," which often asks them
to go along with practices which disturb them or may have
effects they would like to study further.

Even the action which grows out of such group reflection
will not drastically change our society, but it should help
us rediscover some neglected Christian values and deepen
our sense of the corporate meaning of salvation. In addition, even routine office procedures take on a more hu-

man dimension after employees come together on their own initiative to understand the way in which their various assignments fit together in a common purpose and develop strategies by which they can take on increasing responsibility for the timing and methods with which these strategies are to be carried out. This may only be a small example, but it underlines the fact that the most knowledgable and significant suggestions and criticisms relating to the conditions of the marketplace will come from those on the firing line, professionally or vocationally involved.

Christians who come together—one would hope on as ecumenical a basis as possible and with the intention of attracting men and women of other faiths, as well as concerned humanists—to examine the meaning of their working lives are inevitably involved in a subtle dialectic in which self-interest can never be the final arbiter. They have every right to be interested in bettering their own conditions, but their analysis begins with the observation of the needs around them; the professional and industry-wide codes, which are the logical outgrowth of such scrutiny, should seek to recapture the idealism of an earlier period of industrial trade unionism.

The example is deliberately chosen, because no amount of religious motivation should make us forget that we are ultimately dealing with the problem of power. Christians should not assume that we are less prone than others to develop rationalizations for our own desire for power. But group self-criticism should constantly keep before us the idea that power is to be shared with the powerless and the oppressed. We have the example of Jesus in the synagogue at Nazareth reading from the scroll of the prophet Isaiah: "He (the Lord) has anointed me to preach good news to the poor. He has sent me to proclaim release to the captives and recovering of sight to the blind, to set at liberty those who are oppressed, to proclaim the acceptable year of the Lord" (Luke 4:18).

THE NEEDS OF THE WORLD

Our growth in an understanding of a Christian sense of
priorities will also serve to widen our horizons. Just as
the family should be a school of generosity preparing to
welcome Christ iñˢthe guest who arrives uninvited, our
understanding of the good of the community should be
especially sensitive to the cries of "the wretched of the
earth." In theory, the internationalism of Roman Catholicism should be a resource for all Christians who wish to
avoid the idolatry of the nation; in practice, a defensive
mentality derived from recent immigrant status has left too
many Catholics victims of the false patriotism which leaves
no room for claims that would transcend national self-
interest. Fortunately, ecologists are reminding us that we
are responsible for all of creation, and an increasing number of families are finding that better nutrition can be
logically joined to citizen support for a group like Bread
for the World. As we saw before, good intentions will not
suffice, but the technical studies and expert testimony on
international affairs can build on our informed observation
of overall needs.

When it comes to the needs of the world, we would do
well to keep before us the declaration of Dom Helder
Camara, the heroic archbishop of Recife, Brazil: "The
first world is the problem." Sober analysts like Barbara
Ward have for years been trying to dramatize the fact that
the white, post-colonial, post-Christian minority who live
in North America and Europe consume each year over 70
percent of the world's wealth, although they make up less
than 20 percent of the world's people. Have we yet understood that she is pointing out the scale of our obligations
in justice? Has it yet occurred to us that when we ask God
to hasten the Kingdom in the Lord's Prayer, we are logically pledging ourselves to struggle for a world in which
the United States—and the other powerful industrial na-

tions of the world, including Russia—is less able to control international trade and the prices of raw materials, and perhaps even less able to provide each of us with our own automobile?

By now some may suspect that the demands of faith have none too subtly been reduced to social activism. That this is a danger in practice, I could hardly deny, but my first concern is that our response to the gospel be more than the repetition of a creedal or devotional formula. Catholic organized lay activity has been built upon the basis of small-group gospel inquiries related to observation of needs in one's student, family/neighborhood, and work environment. It should be clear that the kind of commitment to the secular world for which I have been pleading will not survive beyond a short season of faddish enthusiasm or it will be corrupted by the disappointments and egoism that accompany such a struggle for change unless it is joined to a constantly deepened life of prayer. Fortunately, recent pronouncements from both Roman Catholic and Protestant sources have encouraged us to see the spiritual unity in just such an endeavor.

The Second Vatican Council, for example, gives this description of the role of the laity in its *Constitution on the Church* (1965): "These faithful are by baptism made one body with Christ and are established among the people of God. They are in their own way made sharers in the priestly, prophetic and kingly functions of Christ. They carry out their own part in the mission of the whole Christian people with respect to the Church and the world." Even earlier, at the Third Assembly of the World Council of Churches at New Delhi (1961), the final report on the laity declares: "Within this whole enterprise of corporate witness, every individual Christian will play his own unique part according to the gifts of the Spirit with which he is endowed. . . . It is obvious that, if the Christian witness is to penetrate into all those areas where the work of the world is carried on, it must be carried there by laymen.

They alone can bring Christian judgment to bear upon all
the issues of life in the spheres of industry and commerce,
scientific research and social organization, and all the other
activities which make up the workaday world. Their meet-
ing-points in the secular world can become real opportunities for the witness of a living Church in the midst of
the busy world's life."

AN AUTHENTIC LAY RESPONSE

Surely lay people who respond to such invitations will
be the first to recognize their own need for ongoing Christian formation. Only a Biblical witness nourished in the
community of the church can join the habit of mental
prayer to a discernment of the action of the Spirit in the
signs of the times. Its product will be an authentically lay
response, not one determined by even the most enlightened
of denominational central committees or episcopal conferences. What is important here is not any ideological
anticlericalism or adolescent rebellion against legitimate
authority but the ability to lay our own gift on the altar.

Realism dictates that we keep in mind Jan Grootaers'
suggestion that "If we wish to systematize the history of
the Roman Catholic Church in the simplest possible way,
we might say that it is the history of the tension between
the institutional and the prophetic elements in the Church.
The history of the layman has been very largely the history
of the prophetic element."

We are still suffering from an interpretation of Christ's
call for more laborers to gather the harvest as meaning that
more people should go to theological seminaries or enter
monasteries. His "vineyard," however, is not another name
for the church but an image of the kingdom we should all
be praying and preparing for. A teaching which implies a
higher spirituality to be practiced by religious professionals
leaves the rest of us free to "get ahead" in the good old
American way, as long as we use the weekly collection

envelopes that have been thoughtfully left in the pews.

Ivan Illich's argument that there are too many full-time workers in the ecclesiastical institution, too many priests and ministers, should be understood as liberating rather than threatening. His point is that only with the depletion of its clerical ranks will the church be forced to free itself of the cultural accretions which obscure its fundamental mission. What is called for is the development of communities of adult Christians meeting together around a table in small groups of extended families.

In an area of Brazil north of Rio de Janeiro the country people were consulted in the preparation of a brief statement on "The Church We Want" (*Cross Currents,* Spring 1976). After calling for a church that would be the people of God, a community church, Christ-centered, ecumenical and dynamic, prophetic and liberating, they asked for a church of lay people: "The church is the ordinary faithful, men and women. Certain lay people have become priests or have been named bishops or chosen popes, not in order to give commands, but in order to serve the community of the faithful. Pope John XXIII was a poor Italian peasant. The church is formed by all those who believe. But it is not enough to know that one belongs to a family; one must take up one's place in it and feel responsible for the growth of that family. Lay people ought more and more to have their voice in the councils of the church, since they are the church."

This seems to me a church which most of us would be glad to make our own.

Sally Cunneen *

5.

Vocation for Women Today

THE RELATIONSHIP OF WOMEN'S EXPERI-
ence to the life of faith and of the church is not an academic one for me. Both have been of great importance in
my life, strengthening me through the sacraments and
idealism in time of adolescence, helping me accept the
reality of the death of parents and a son as an adult. But
although I was always a believing Christian and a regular
churchgoer, as a wife and mother some fifteen years ago
I began to feel a growing tension between the spiritual advice I received from the pulpit and the actual decisions I
had to make as a wife, mother, and citizen. They simply
did not connect, and I felt cut off from a necessary source
of life.

I began to question other women, both Protestant and
Catholic like myself, and discovered they too felt both in
and out of the church and were anxious to explore the

* SALLY CUNNEEN is associate editor of *Cross Currents* and an
editor-at-large of *Christian Century*. She is also the author of *Sex:
Female; Religion: Catholic* and *A Contemporary Meditation on
the Everyday Good*.

reasons. My conversations grew into an extensive survey and eventually a book on the changing attitudes of Catholic women to their place in church and society. I would like first to review some of the feelings I encountered among these women at that time, for I believe that reflection on them reveals they have something to say to all of us who care about the role of the laity and the direction the church takes today.

Many tensions surfaced in their correspondence. Besides the obvious conflict of the conscientious married woman who felt a moral obligation to use birth control when official teaching said no, there was a frequent complaint that no way existed for women—or for lay men either—to participate in the community of the church. Single women faced acute problems, perhaps most forcefully expressed by an older woman: "It becomes more and more difficult to be patient and understanding when one is treated as an equal in the professional and intellectual secular world but as a second-class citizen in one's own church. Just for the record, I don't want to be a priest, but I want to make that choice myself and not have it made for me." And finally, a nun from Montreal summed up the feeling of many women who were sisters when she said, "I don't feel that I have been given the same priority as a man to be really 'in' the church. I would like to feel that theologically my womanhood was really important to the church, that it had a place."

Such feelings (like my own) were always accompanied, however, by strong statements of love for the church and a determination to stay in it. Perhaps women had to redefine it a little to include their own needs and hopes: they tended to see it less as institution and more as an ecumenical community of believers. One elderly woman expressed the overall attitude fairly well: "Despite my criticism, I think the church is the hope of our world. But this will only become apparent when it sees its mission to help people live humanly now, as soon as possible; when it forgets the ab-

stract preaching and tries to feed, clothe, and educate the
people of God, all three billion of them."

PERSONAL FREEDOM AND SOCIAL JUSTICE

And so I discovered some twelve years ago that two
powerful desires were surfacing among believing women:
first, they wished to be freer (from early childhood) to
develop without the restrictions of socially imposed roles
and images. They were sick and tired of being told in
church, for example, that they were selfless "by nature"
and destined to live only through and for others. And second, that the church should see its task as service to all
of God's family, especially the poorest. Personal freedom
and social justice. No pressure from society and total dedication to it. I sensed a certain contradiction here, a gap
between these two desires I felt myself. How could we be
sure that if we freely defined ourselves we would still be
Christians and church members? Was there not an element
of egoism and selfishness here that might prevent it? And if
we as parents and educators really encouraged free self-
development among the young, fostering their self-confi-
dence, how could we be sure they would choose service
to the handicapped rather than success as a rock star at
the other end of the process? There seemed, in my mind,
no logical connection between the two poles of desire. Over
the intervening years, however, I have found some evidence
that they are in fact connected. And it is my slow discovery
of the nature of this union I want to explore next.

FROM SELFISHNESS TOWARD SERVICE

One of the first women I interviewed twelve years ago
underlined the split between the two desires. Since she
was both founder and spokeswoman of a nonviolent peace
movement and a courageous worker for prisoners and victims of injustice around the world, I already knew of her

social commitment. I was stunned, however, at her response to my question as to how we could best pass on our religious values to young women today. Without hesitation she answered in her firm, ladylike tone: "Build up their egos."

At the time I was not clear enough in my own mind to push on to the next question that would have explored the contradiction. Only several years later when my experience with the energy and confusion of women's groups became more practical and less theoretical, did I receive a key.

I had long been impressed by the life and work of a friend of mine, a mother and writer whose own concern for her brain-damaged child had led her in stages to develop a local network of volunteers and professionals into organizations on behalf of many "special" children. The spirit and success of these organizations, which neither wasted money nor excluded anyone who needed help (many did not fit into one or another of the bureaucratic categories set up by public agencies) prompted me to ask her for the secret of her ability to mobilize and maintain support for some of the most hidden of the neediest among us. "Just two things," she replied. "First, let people love themselves a little. Appeal to the goodness in them, not the guilt. Then show them a practical way to help other people who truly need it."

APPEAL TO THE GOD IN PERSONS

It is hard to believe how well this advice works in practice, and it would be even harder to explain how much human understanding it contains. It also holds the clue to the contradiction I had met among women, and I realized it when I came across the personal odyssey of Joan Bel Geddes, who spelled out its meaning in terms of her life experience ("Charity Really Does Begin at Home—With the Self," *Holiness and Mental Health,* Paulist Press, 1972). She spoke of herself there as a classic case of definition by others, the state I found women complained of most frequently as a source of self-alienation in later life.

Perhaps this convert to Catholicism from a basically nonreligious background paid too much attention to her religious mentor's advice on how to be the ideal religious woman. Most of us were able to ignore or temper it with other influences. But she is all the more revealing on the limitations of what used to be rather typical advice. Taking to heart the suggested need for self-denial and the ideal of service to others, Joan adopted a regime that strove for perfection in all details, except that she failed to take into consideration the actual person God had made her by birth. The more she tried to reach the perfection of selfless service, the more she saw her natural temper getting shorter and the harder she had to work to overcome her faults. Her painful self-discovery, coming only after the breakup of her marriage reveals the wisdom of my friend's advice: people need to love themselves a little before they can help others.

In a therapy group, Joan slowly came to see herself more clearly with all her quirks and limitations, but with God-given stamina and sharpness of vision as well as a saving sense of humor. When she stopped concentrating on the evil in herself she had to get rid of, she began developing the human strengths she needed. She began to like herself a little, and as she did she found she liked other people better, too, and that she could pray as she never had before.

Joan found her therapy group quite different in its methods from her spiritual guide. Its members were sometimes brutally frank, but they taught her to know when she was kidding herself and when she was being too hard on herself, and she experienced their care as Christian love. We are asked as Christians to love our neighbor as ourselves, Joan reminds us, but often we neglect ourselves, so that service to our neighbor is neither spontaneously loving nor effective. Yet it is in and through the people we actually are that we must live our Christianity today. How different is this attitude of self as a medium from its absence among the young would-be nuns a Mother Superior described to me with dry humor some years ago: "So many of them show up here all whipped up to work for God, but not one of them with any idea how!"

Loving ourselves a little, coming to know ourselves and others, then we can also see how we might find our way to work for and with them. Joan's story showed me that growth in personal responsibility was the middle point between the pole of freedom and the pole of service in women's desires. Through it, one went from one to the other. And many nuns today, like other believing women, have come to search out their vocations in the realistic interaction of their natural attitudes and the needs and possibilities around them. The knowledge that human maturity is the way to obedience is what is needed today.

TOWARD TRUE MATURITY

Although we tend to forget it sometimes, recalling the story of his love for little children, Jesus always offered those around him a challenge that required human strength and maturity. He stressed the need to depart from one's own natural family, at least psychologically: "He who loves father or mother more than me is not worthy of me." And he spoke of the heavy responsibility his followers must assume: "He who does not take up his cross and follow me is not worthy of me." These are hard words, and it is important to remember that Jesus was perhaps the most mature human being who ever lived. The psychologist C. G. Jung saw him as the model of the fully realized human person. Competent to separate himself from his own family and the pressure of social and religious custom he was able to discover his own divine mission. Then Jesus returned and mediated the message of the Father to all those who would listen. His strength carried him through ridicule, the loss of followers, and finally, a disgraceful death in obedience to his call.

And surely his mother Mary was a tower of human strength as well. As a child I used to place flowers before a cool statue in blue whose hands stretched out, palms up, in a gesture of resigned submission. As an adult I believe that the real Mary would not have recognized herself in that statue. This is not the young woman who made a difficult journey to visit her pregnant cousin Elizabeth, proclaiming, "He has brought down monarchs from their thrones but the humble have been lifted high." It was not docility that kept Mary faithful through all the unexpected implications of her consent; only loving courage could have helped her through the trial and crucifixion of her Son, and creative commitment was necessary to support his outlawed community when he was gone.

TOWARD TRUE STRENGTH

More than ever today we need some of that strength if we are to be Christian. All of us need it to endure the pain and suffering that comes inevitably to us and to those we love. But we need it for more active purposes, too. Women had been complaining precisely because they found that passivity, docility, was not a virtue which helped them live morally in a world radically different in some ways from that in which Jesus lived. Perhaps the difference between that world and ours can be grasped if we try to answer the question Jesus raised with his story of the good Samaritan: who is my neighbor? I mentioned earlier the response to one woman who referred quite simply to the whole human family. Surely the presence of jet planes and television news has made us aware of the existence as people of tribes and nations that were merely exotic names when we were children. It has also taught us that what we and they grow or eat or use for power intimately affects the other.

Unlike the Samaritan who found one man injured and lying by the side of his path, we are faced with multiple neighbors whose needs are visible to us—a starving tribe in Africa, flood victims in Pennsylvania, drug addicts in our nearest city. And their needs, equally demanding, may often conflict, not only in terms of the limits of our pocket-book, but in actually calling for attitudes or votes that pit one group of neighbors against another. In some cases, such as the equally valid claims of teenagers, women, old persons, or migrants for a small number of jobs, we may find those giving pitted against those who must receive.

We know about such social conflicts and how difficult it is to be a good neighbor today. Increasingly we have turned to agencies and institutions. Yet we have also come to know that agencies do not necessarily act as good Samaritans even when the people in them are honest individuals. They tend to become impersonal and at times even to dehumanize those they serve. As individual Christians, then, we seem faced with the call to be good neighbors to many people we simply do not know how to help effectively.

NEW HOPE AND PROMISE

It is easy to lose both hope and direction in such complex, even contradictory circumstances. But perhaps because I am a woman and feel I have gone through a process beginning in just such conflicts in my own life, I feel that the present is nevertheless a time of promise for Christianity such as it has not known since the days of the early church. For the very limits of the earth's resources reveal to us our interdependence on one another, and this is a challenge to us to relate ourselves wherever or whoever we are to the human struggles around the globe that such limits necessitate.

When I look for an example, I think first of a housewife who lives across the Hudson River from me. A few years ago we both read in the paper that the amount of humanly edible protein fed to American livestock and not returned for human consumption approached the whole world's protein deficit. I deplored the fact and pigeonholed it in my mind; Frances Moore Lappé asked herself, "Is this necessary?" She then took it upon herself to find out that it was not. She also discovered sensible ways to avoid such waste. Several years and two children after posing the initial question to herself, she came out with *Diet for a Small Planet*. This remarkable little book provides the rest of us with information about food production and nutrition that enables us in Hackensack or Houston to buy, cook, and eat food that will nourish us and will not decrease the possibility of well-being among people who inhabit the other side of the globe.

The earth and human history are themselves calling us to greater interdependence today. Partly perhaps because they have not been in established power positions in the old way of running things, women are among the most vocal in hailing this new interdependence and in finding creative ways to implement it. This is true on the interpersonal level.

I think of a friend of mine, a mother and psychologist, who, after years of struggling with her own and others' family conflicts, has discovered a way to cope with them equably: she recommends a declaration of interdependence. This attitude extends to the public sphere, however, and should dispel the fears of those who believe that the entrance of women into public life will be harmful to them, their families or society. Of course, immature or insensitive people can always avoid the obligations of home and family and justify it by "doing good," men as well as women.

We meet such a character in Dickens' *Bleak House* when we visit the Jellyby home. In a chapter aptly entitled "Telescopic Philanthropy" we see the children first. Wearing dirty clothes, they are playing around the house and on the street, one little boy with his head stuck between the fence posts and another who falls down stairs. Mrs. Jellyby doesn't notice, being a "lady of very remarkable strength of character, who devotes herself entirely to the public." Her intense concern for the development of the natives of Borrioboola-Gha is such that it enables her to remain oblivious to the crying needs of husband, household, and children.

SOME GLOBAL CONCERNS

Such blindness to one's own motives and surroundings, however, is worlds apart from what the women of whom I speak represent. Their concern is precisely to relate personal and nearby reality to more remote human needs. Unless such connections can be made, we will remain unable to argue effectively against the spread of such current evils as looting, vandalism, corporate thievery, and even genocide. The thrust of this connection arises not from our urge to "do good" to others, but simply in facing the reality that we are all sharers on this small spaceship earth.

One woman who helps us see the implications of this global interdependence most clearly is Barbara Ward, who shaped her own life's work into a powerful plea for human relatedness across national barriers. Former foreign affairs editor of the *London Economist* and a Governor of the British Broadcasting Corporation, she turned more and more to preaching the gospel of our economic interdependence in her widely influential books and lectures. Speaking of the tendency of rich nations to ignore the increasing gap between their income and that of the poor nations she asks: Can we let Lazarus sit at the gate? We need to develop a human economics, a human morality, instead of those we now have which are based on private and national moralities.

At the same time that she analyses the very real economic problems we face as world citizens, Barbara Ward tells us that we can do something about them through our actions as citizens and consumers. She, too, gives us a "way" to relate and, moreover, she reminds us that faith is intimately connected with her thirst for human justice. In helping us see that in our world religion is relevant to the hopes and aspirations of humanity, Barbara Ward confirms Pope John's prophetic view of the meaning of women's contribution to the modern world.

In the first papal encyclical ever written to all the peoples of the earth, *Pacem in Terris,* John pointed out three signs of the new era the world was entering, one of them being the desire of women for free and responsible participation in determining their own lives "in the social and economic sphere, in the fields of learning and culture, and in public life." The common task to which they and all people are called by the Lord to dedicate themselves now, he believed, was "the task of restoring the human family in truth, in justice, in love, and in freedom." Like Frances Lappé and Barbara Ward, Pope John was well aware that the problem to which religion as well as public policy must address itself was the fact that many groups of people are not free, economically or psychologically. Those who are in a position to think about helping them must now remember that the participation of those they hope to help—no matter how inarticulate—is nevertheless essential in determining the nature of that help.

CONCEPT OF PERSON

Note the twofold emphasis here again on self-definition as well as social progress. In calling attention to their own desire for self-definition, it seems, women represented every group which has been, for whatever reason, defined by others. This was what Pope John realized. When they have come to define themselves, the word I have heard Christian women use is equally applicable to all: "person." Sometimes in the press it is used as a neutral, almost joking term. Yet "person" has become a powerful, positive term in the aspirations of religious women. As they use it, the word describes the human at a deep level beneath external differences, and it implies inner participation in one's outer destiny. When some women felt that "woman" as a definition was being used to mean "other" or "lesser," they dug a little deeper within themselves and encountered the "person." This basic identity does not deny female sexuality, but it refuses to be defined totally by it.

The concept of "person" has become central in the thinking of women theologians. Virginia Mollenkott's *Women, Men, and the Bible,* for example, describes the "mutual submission of persons" as the recommended Biblical model for all relationships. It prevents us from using others as objects; it bars all master-slave relations. To let one's sex override one's humanity is indeed to be a materialist and a determinist, not a Christian, Mollenkott points out. She believes that in calling attention to the Christian, personal way of relating, Christian feminists are calling the churches back to their own central teaching and to the possibility of relating their private virtues to their public behavior.

I find her belief in the healing nature of women's testimony amply fulfilled in the theological stance of a collective statement made in 1975 by a group of Catholic women, lay and religious. In answer to a request by the American Catholic bishops for recommendations on the role of women in church and society, this Task Force outlined some down-to-earth suggestions but first stated the theological grounds on which they made them:

The Church must affirm a new order based on certain basic faith convictions regarding the person, the mission of the ecclesial community, and the gifts of the spirit. Every human being is caught up in the "one great act of giving birth" which leads to the fullness of "freedom of the children of God" (Rom. 8:21–22). That is, every human being is engaged in a living process of becoming liberated as a complete human

being, of becoming wholly human, touching and touched by
God. Since every person is called to this liberation of the
spirit, she/he possesses an inherent right to these opportunities,
goods, and services—be they relational, psychological, spiritual
—necessary for full development as a person.

While the person is thus called to wholeness, the Church—
the communion of persons gathered to remember and follow
Jesus—is itself responding to a mission; to proclaim the reign
of God, to help every person discover the reign within, and
to prepare the way for its full blossoming in justice and peace.[1]

Paradoxically, having become free enough to define
themselves, the women who wrote this statement exhibit
just those nurturing qualities we have tended to call feminine and even maternal. One must of course be strong to
live them. The mother who is strong reaches out to the
child who is weak and yet never thinks of him as an inferior being, but rather as the independent adult he can
become. And the essence of the mother-child relationship
is the personal; no society, however efficient or constructive or rational, can find a substitute for intimacy any more
than it can find a replacement for food and drink. We
remember that Christ spoke of the hireling who flees when
the wolf comes because he has no personal concern for
the sheep. The change that has occurred in the climate of
our consciousness is such that the nun I mentioned earlier
would now feel that her femininity *was* theologically important to the church. In our increasingly impersonal world,
all of us know that the compassionate qualities of "the
feminine" are as necessary in public and ecclesial life as
are the strengths of "the masculine" in private life, and
that both these qualities must be combined to some extent
in each of us.

This insistence on retaining personal quality in all our
relationships is important because it casts new light on
how members of local churches see each other. It reminds
us that our deepest relationship is to one another as people—that is, as laity—and that this voluntary commitment
to one another in the service of Christ as human beings

precedes any divisions that age or sex or office or vocation may make. Part of our vocation as laity, in fact, may be to remind the ecclesial community of this reality. This was certainly true of the Mexican-American widow and community worker who exclaimed to the bishops at their open hearing as to what concerned the people in the church in San Antonio: "How can there be a universal church if the root of the tree that is to give fruit is not a priority within the church?"

Many lay people, of course, have not been accustomed to think that they are the church. Yet there is among them a hunger to relate the word of the Lord to the transactions of their daily lives. Exploring the questions—even the conflicts and contradictions—that arise from this experience would yield rich harvests to preachers whose own veins have run dry. Indeed, short honest talks from parishioners might well be the means of mature Christian development for all members of the local church.

Where laity are silent from long habit, facilitators (not "experts") from within the community can help them to talk more freely about the doubts and contradictions they hold. Trust and vision will grow as people in the local church come to know each other. Of course, certain notions of authority may change when groups like these increase, but what is lost will be arid compared to the life that is gained. From my experience, I would say that it will revivify the sense of office rather than destroy it.

At the same time, local churches will be freer to try many things because they will no longer confuse themselves with the kingdom of God but rather see themselves as human mediators of the Holy Spirit in the real world of chaos and death. Free to fail, to bear with one another, to try again. Free, too, to work with others aiding human growth. Encouraging the independence of its own members, it will point to the value of social interdependence as well. As theologian Rodger Van Allen reminds us, "All are called to a life led by the Spirit, not one that presumes on the Spirit." Although Van Allen, too, sees the present moment as one of crisis for the church, he believes that ecclesial identity based on commitment to a serious lay vocation may make the crisis a source of "renewed appreciation of the fundamental nature of Christian vocation and fellowship. If this happens, we will be well on the way to uncovering a way of life that is more integral for the person, and more concerned with the quality of human life." [2]

As local churches come to see the centrality of the lay identity and vocation, they will find their mission as church changes too, for religion becomes a vital factor in personal growth and social life. The lay vocation refocuses the center of ecclesial attention away from institutional and theoretical concerns toward human life and God's creation. In so doing it reveals the relevance of religion to ecology, to rational use of energy, indeed, to the human project. The degree to which the potential mission becomes real, however, depends on the vision and efforts of individuals in response to the Spirit. This is the task that faces us as laity today and calls for all our ingenuity as well as faith and hope.

NOTES

1. From the unpublished Bishop's Task Force Report on Women in Church and Society. Many of its recommendations found their way into the actions voted on in Detroit, November, 1977, at the "Call to Action" assembly.

2. *Cross Currents,* a quarterly review to explore the implication of Christianity for our times, Convergence, Inc., West Nyack, New York, Volume XXII, Spring, 1972.

From Personal
toward Corporate

Richard J. Mouw *

6.

The Corporate
Calling of the Laity

ON A LOCALLY-PRODUCED TELEVISION
program a few years ago four businessmen discussed the
topic, "The Christian in the World of Business." (I use the
word "business*men*" here advisedly—they were all males.
An equally crucial topic would be, "The Christian Woman
in the Male-Dominated World of Business.") The first
three panelists expressed what were in effect variations on
the same theme. The world of business, they told us, is full
of tensions and frustrations. In such a context they have
found it necessary to draw on the "inner resources" which
the Christian faith provides. As one of them put it: "I don't
know how I would survive in the dog-eat-dog world of
business if I couldn't regularly get away from it all in
order to spend some time alone with the Lord."

The fourth panelist introduced a new note: "All of this

* DR. RICHARD J. MOUW is a professor of philosophy at Calvin
College, Grand Rapids, Michigan, and is the author of two books,
Political Evangelism and *Politics and Biblical Drama*. Dr. Mouw
is an active layman who is a leader in the evangelical cluster of
churches.

talk about 'peace of mind' and 'alone with the Lord' is
fine. But I'm an insurance agent, and I want to know how
to bring the Lord *into* my business. What does it mean for
me to write up a policy *as* a Christian? How am I to differ
from others in my understanding of what it means to 'make
a good deal'? Those are the questions which I struggle
with—and so far I haven't gotten a lot of help in finding
answers." And in spite of the fact that the discussion turned
to the role of "personal values" in business practices, it
was obvious that the answers were not forthcoming on this
particular program.

The comments which follow here will have the concerns
of this insurance agent in mind. This does not mean that
we will specify what would go into the making of a "Christian insurance policy." But we will pursue the topic of the
corporate responsibilities of Christian laity with his request
for guidance in mind. As someone who deals with the
theological and philosophical foundations of Christian
social action, it is helpful, on occasion, to be forced to
apply such reflections to the complexities of a specific form
of corporate involvement.

Indeed, I suspect that we will not develop an adequate
theology of and for the laity until we get beyond general
talk about "the laity" and begin addressing the specific
concerns of the insurance agent, the waitress, the farmer,
and the florist. This is not to say that the theologian or
the philosopher or the preacher can address these concerns
simply by "giving answers" to the kinds of questions asked
by our insurance agent. There is an important sense in
which we must wait for some answers from him before we
can begin looking for the guidance he has requested. And
this, in turn, must be one part of a very lengthy conversation that will include not only insurance agents and theologians but also economists, dentists, supermarket cashiers,
and unemployed persons. But more about this conversation further on.

THE COMPLEXITIES OF THE GOSPEL

Our insurance agent has raised some important concerns about the role of the Christian in the world of business. But what about his fellow-panelists? We must not
give the impression that the other three businessmen were
talking about matters that are silly or misguided. They
discussed their Christian experience in very personal terms
and there is nothing intrinsically wrong with that kind of
talk. Christianity is not *merely* a personal religion, but
it is *at least* a personal religion. A commitment to Jesus
Christ does, or ought to, provide us with "inner resources."
It does, or ought to, bring us "peace" in times of frustration and tension. Such matters ought not to be belittled or
derided. On the contrary, we ought to rejoice in the fact
that a firm trust in the God of the Scriptures regularly
brings serenity, discipline, and a sense of integrity into the
personal lives of business executives—or teachers, parents,
legislators, and priests, for that matter.

The question of how we can best integrate the personal
and corporate aspects of the Christian gospel has been an
explicit matter of concern recently in many segments of
the Christian community. Evangelical Protestants have had
a strong tendency to emphasize the personal elements to the
exclusion of a concern with dealing with corporate structures as such. Liberal Protestants, especially those in the
tradition of the "social gospel," have emphasized the corporate almost to the exclusion of the personal dimensions.
A similar tension exists between two important movements within post-Vatican-II Roman Catholicism—the neo-
charismatic renewal and Latin-American-based liberation
theologies.

In recent years, however, many Christians have refused
to accept these polarizations as inevitable, with the result
that there seems to be an emerging quest for a more

"holistic" Christianity in which there is a concern for both personal and corporate change. The need to integrate the personal and corporate dimensions can be explained and justified in several ways. For one thing, it is not as easy to draw hard and fast lines between the "personal" and the "corporate" as it is sometimes thought to be. Were the President's misdeeds in the Watergate affair "personal" or "corporate" ones?

But even where meaningful boundaries can be drawn there are still strong connections between personal and corporate activity. Suppose we were to attempt to set up an evangelism program in an all-black neighborhood in the hope that we could encourage individual persons to "accept Christ as personal Savior." If some of them could not read our literature because of inadequate reading programs in the local schools, wouldn't we begin to be concerned about the quality of inner-city education? Or suppose someone refuses to talk to us because his landlord, who will not make necessary repairs on his rental property, is a member of our church? If we were really serious about this kind of "personal evangelism," it would become obvious to us that we have our work cut out for us, and that this work necessitates attention to the corporate structures which affect the lives of black city-dwellers.

This is to say that a concern for individual persons ought to be rooted in a concern about the corporate structures in whose context individuals live. But the argument also moves in the opposite direction. A concern for corporate change must also be grounded in a concern for personal change. One of the ironies of the anti-war movement of the 1960s was that many of the young people who believe that the differences between Washington and Hanoi could be resolved if only both sides would "give peace a chance" viewed their differences of opinion with their own parents as hopelessly irreconcilable.

Properly understood, personal and corporate concerns

exist on a continuum—and it is impossible to separate them in a neatly compartmentalized manner. Theologically, the interrelationships can be viewed on three levels. First, individual and corporate phenomena are both part of the *creation*. God creates human beings as individuals—"male and female created he them"—and he commands them to have "dominion" over the earth that he has made (Gen. 1:26–31). This command includes the mandate to engage in "culture"—building activities—in H. Richard Niebuhr's sense of "culture" as the "artificial" or "secondary environment" which it is necessary to construct if we are to "fill" and "subdue" the earth. In this sense then, corporate structures—institutions, organizations, decision-making patterns, codified expectations, and the like—are instruments of shared human responsibility. And the Scriptures insist that they can be *good* instruments: they can serve as a means whereby the love of God and neighbor is facilitated.

Second, both individual and corporate phenomena can come under the rule of *sin*. Sin begins as personal rebellion, as an acceptance of the serpent's promise that we can be our own gods. But corporate structures—those institutions, organizations, patterns, and codes which could have functioned as elements in the good creation—take on the character of our personal rebellions. They become extensions, even counterparts, of our sinful selves, and because they come to embody human rebellion, it is possible to speak of "corporate sin" or "institutional sin."

Third, both individual and corporate phenomena are within the scope of the *redemption* that has been brought about by the atoning work of Jesus Christ. In the Old Testament, God's redemptive activity was obviously directed toward the creation of a people, a nation, in whose corporate life the divine *shalom* would be revealed—so that all of the peoples of the earth could see what it is like for people to live, both individually and collectively, in obedience to the will of the Creator of humankind. And this pattern does not change in the New Testament; here, too, God calls into existence a people: "Once you were no people but now you are God's people" (1 Peter 2:10)— to serve as a model of individual and collective obedience under the Lordship of Christ.

Both the Israelite nation of the Old Testament and the church as the New Testament Israel, then, are "show-piece" communities, the means by which God reveals his creating purposes in the world. But God's called-out community is also meant to function as an *agent* of his redemptive work. We, as Christians, are not merely called to *be* a community, but also to act *upon* other communities and structures in the hope of rescuing them from the injustice and unrighteousness of sin.

This task of functioning as redemptive agents cannot be properly pursued unless we recognize the reality of the "corporate sin" to which we have already referred. One way in which some Christians have attempted to find a short-cut in this area is expressed in the popular Christian slogan, "Changed hearts will change society." There is a grain of truth in this slogan. Changed hearts, if they are properly changed, will surely *want* to change unjust structures and unrighteous patterns. But it is misleading to suggest that by "changing hearts" through evangelistic efforts we will automatically bring about the elimination of corporate injustice.

Consider again our example about evangelism in the inner city. It is possible for a black Christian ghetto-dweller to rent a slum home from a white Christian landlord without eliminating the evil perpetuated by unjust housing standards. Similarly we could "convert" all of the teachers and all of the students in a given inner-city school and still have poor reading-education programs—to get at the rest of this problem we must deal with tax allocations, textbook revision, teacher training, collective expectations, and so on.

And this is where we left our insurance agent. He wanted to know how to bring Christ *into* his business. Inner strength, peace of mind, moments alone with God—all of these things are fine, but they leave relatively untouched the "dog-eat-dog world of business." What about large insurance companies who insist that he charge higher rates to insure people in poorer neighborhoods? How can he compete with other agents who are willing to use dishonest tactics? What is an "honest" margin of profit? What about overselling to rich customers in order to undercharge poorer customers? When is it proper to say, "Well, that's the kind of thing you have to do in a sinful world"?

Our insurance agent's questions illustrate the point we have been making: the Christian gospel is a complex message. It is a message which speaks to us in all aspects of our lives: as emotional and sexual beings, as playing and working beings, as political and worshiping beings. It is a message of good news for both individual life and corporate involvement. It is a message that comes to us in a world that is not only created, but fallen, and not only fallen, but redeemable.

CORPORATE RESOURCES

I was once asked to help lead a discussion on "the Gospel and the Poor" for a group of Christians made up of persons from the business community. After some brief presentations setting forth the Biblical mandate to identify with the needs of the poor, we had a freewheeling discussion. This conversation was fascinating in that the vocal members of the group began by arguing that there really *isn't* all that much poverty in North America. Two of my fellow discussion leaders were members of minority races, and they succeeded in rebutting this thesis very effectively. At a point exactly halfway through the discussion, the opposition shifted arguments and proceeded to insist that things were *so* bad that there is little we can do about it, short of hoping for the return of Christ.

In short, this group of business leaders was willing to

accept either one of two conflicting viewpoints: one being that things are not very bad and so there is little that we as Christians *need* to do; and the other being that things are so very bad that there is little that we as Christians *can* do. The one viewpoint which they seemed to be unwilling to accept is this one: that things are quite bad, but that nonetheless we as Christians should be trying to change the situation.

Since the two acceptable viewpoints lead, for different reasons, to inaction, whereas the unacceptable perspective is precisely the one that requires active involvement in the plight of the poor, it seems fair to assume that this particular group had strong, but unstated, reasons for noninvolvement in this area of concern. Why? What were the reasons?

One can think of some uncharitable explanations. It is easy to accuse well-to-do and middle class church members of an antipoor bias or of a desire to protect the "vested interests" appropriate to their economic stations. But this is, I think, *too* easy. In many cases it is more proper to locate the basic cause in a strong sense of personal inadequacy on the part of many laypersons. They resist active involvement because they are unclear as to what active involvement will require of them.

And why *shouldn't* the laity experience feelings of inadequacy when it comes to efforts to change corporate structures? Remember our insurance agent's complaint: "Those are the questions which I struggle with—and so far I haven't gotten a lot of help in finding the answers." Even where there is a willingness, the way is not very clear. Church leaders, at their best, have insisted that the laity bring Christian principles to bear on their vocations, but they have offered little concrete guidance as to how this is to be done. At their worst, the leaders have made it clear that they have their own identity crises to deal with. In all of this, we should not be surprised if the laity feel that they are inadequate to do what they are sometimes told to do.

We can understand something of the frustration which our insurance agent is experiencing. He has refused to suppress his conviction that being a Christian ought to influence his understanding of the corporate structures within which he operates. But he does not have the resources to answer all of the difficult questions on his own. His minister or priest, as the case may be, knows little about the world of business. When our businessman turns to his Christian colleagues, they want to limit the conversation to the topic of "inner peace." To whom can he go?

It is possible to picture the place at which the help must be given. Each Sunday our insurance agent goes to church where he gathers with other followers of Jesus Christ for worship. Here he listens to the preaching of the Word, he participates in sacramental acts, and he offers prayers of petition and thanksgiving. The worship experience is not especially designed for insurance agents; it is meant to bring together people from many areas of concern and activity into a setting in which they affirm their common identity as Christian disciples.

At the close of the worship service, our insurance agent hears a benediction pronounced. Usually this involves a mandate that he go forth from the church into the world as a servant of Jesus with the promise that the triune God will go with him to bless his labors. What our insurance agent is being told at this point is that he must go to his office and attempt to bring the gospel to bear on the matters which people care about in insurance agencies. And he is promised the blessing and comfort of the Creator of the world as he engages in this attempt. Our insurance agent has taken that mandate seriously. But he is confused about how he is to pursue this task.

The question is this: how is he to translate the concerns which he has encountered in the midst of the worshiping throng, on the one hand, into concrete action as someone who writes insurance policies, on the other? Let it be said that there is undoubtedly far more that could be done at each end of this problematic situation than is presently being done. For example, the clergy could surely be making a greater effort at enunciating Biblically grounded principles in relation to various areas of human concern. A minister does not have to be an expert sociologist or political scientist to speak effectively about the sins of racism and sexism. And it is difficult to be sympathetic to the layperson's complaint that no one is offering guidance on political or economic matters when that person has never read an issue of *Christianity and Crisis* or *Commonweal* or *Christianity Today.*

THE GAP BETWEEN WORSHIP AND WORK

Even allowing, however, that there are existing weaknesses *in* both the church and the insurance office, there exists a significant gap *between* the two. What is needed to fill the gap is a rather elaborate conversation which takes place between the two places. "Between" here does not necessarily mean a physical location, for the conversation could take place either in the church or in the office building. The gap is one of *kind* rather than place. It must be filled by a certain sort of educational process, one that cannot take place either in the worship setting or in private study. There is a need for education that bridges the gap between worship and work.

The kind of educational conversation I am proposing should be characterized by at least three features. First, it must be an experience in becoming aware of the *issues* which confront the Christian community, especially in the much neglected areas of social, political, and economic concerns. We might call this the "consciousness-raising" dimension of laity education. This process can take many forms. For one thing, it can include the mutual sharing of the kinds of questions raised by our insurance agent; there should be a forum for him, and others like him, to place questions on the agenda of the Christian community.

But it must also be a conversation in which we hear about concerns which we would not otherwise encounter, even if we were thoroughly familiar with the hopes and fears of others in the worshiping community. For example, if we are accustomed to worshiping and working with middle class whites, then we should have an opportunity to attend to the concerns of the poor, the unemployed, and the politically oppressed. The title of one of Tom Skinner's books expresses the crucial concern here: *If Christ Is the Answer, What Are the Questions?* Christian laity must struggle to get clear about the questions to which answers must be found.

The consciousness-raising of the laity must also include effort to become aware of what our own piety has already committed us to. This is an important item to stress, especially since many Christian activities assume that in order to get "ordinary" Christians involved politically we have to teach them a new theology. But this is not necessarily the case. When we celebrate Christmas by singing that "the hopes and fears of all the years" are met in the birth of Jesus or that "he comes to make his blessings flow far as the curse is found," we have already committed ourselves to a belief that the gospel has political implications. Similarly, when we applaud George Beverly Shea for singing, "I'd rather have Jesus than silver or gold," we have acknowledged the profound economic shape of the Christian message. And when we teach our little children to sing, "Red and yellow, black and white, they are precious in His sight," we have already issued a declaration about race relations. Much Christian consciousness-raising should consist in becoming aware of that to which we have already committed ourselves.

Second, the kind of educational conversation I am proposing must include efforts in the area of *theological* education. Once we are aware of the questions, we must decide just *how* "Christ is the answer." And this necessarily involves theological reflection. There is simply no way around

this point, nor is there any way to avoid the insistence that
to provide the proper kind of theological education for the
laity will require major new efforts on the part of both
laity and church leadership. The laity needs a theological
training which is not merely a "simplified" version of clergy
education. The task will provide bold and creative efforts
to develop theological and educational frameworks for
equipping laypersons for their own kind of ministry within
corporate structures.

Plato argued in the *Republic* that if there were ever going to be philosopher-kings, then either kings had to become philosophers or philosophers had to become kings.
Similarly, if we are ever going to develop a theology for
insurance agencies, then either theologians will have to
become interested in insurance or insurance agents will
have to become interested in theology—or, preferably,
both. Let us assume that our insurance agent will gain the
kind of theological perspective he needs. What will that
perspective look like?

There are many different dimensions to the theological
enterprise—even among professional theologians speciali-
zation is necessary. To insist, then, that the laity must become theologically minded is not to demand that laypersons
become experts in Biblical criticism or eschatology; for
that matter, we do not even demand that preachers become
experts in these fields. Indeed, the laity need not be theological "experts" in any area of theology. But they must
become theologically *minded*.

At the very least, the laity must become familiar with
the area that we might label, "The theology of corporate
structures." This will require familiarity with the Old Testament prophets and the manner in which they reflected
critically on the economic and political practices of Israel
and its neighbors. Paul's references to "principles and
powers" have served as important data in recent discussions of Biblical perspectives on corporate life; the laity
ought to be familiar with these discussions. Recent ec-

clesiastical and ecumenical declarations—such as the documents of Vatican II, the Chicago Declaration of Evangelical Social Concern, the Hartford Appeal, the Boston Affirmations, and the like—could provide helpful resources for discussion. In short, the laity must read books, discuss ideas in a systematic fashion, and submit to disciplined debate, argument, and mutual correction.

Third, the educational conversation must include a concern with "casuistry," the attempt to bring principles and doctrines to bear on concrete situations and practices. Having engaged in theological study, reflection, and discussion on matters having to do with the nature of institutions —the concept of "property," apocalyptic themes, and the like—our insurance agent must ask what all of this means when he is helping families who are assessing the worth of their possessions, planning for their futures, anticipating purchases, buying homes in urban neighborhoods, and so on.

We are all, of course, casuists already. The problem is that many of us are presently doing our casuistic reflection without the other factors we have mentioned. Many Christians are struggling with the wrong questions or are making decisions in situations which have not been properly submitted to Christian scrutiny. More often than not, the laity have no theology whatsoever to "apply" to their concrete predicaments. We can begin to remedy this situation if we recognize the need for an area of discussion that simply cannot be taken care of by either the clergy or the laity working in isolation. We must begin to provide the laity with corporate resources for their corporate calling.

How could this educational conversation be *structured?* It is important to note that many of the required structures or forums are already in existence; it is a matter of providing these existing structures with the proper context. There are already Christian businessmen's associations, organizations for Christian athletes and Christian airline stewardesses, and Christian political groups. If we add to this list the

various organizations that are affiliated with local congregations—adult Sunday school classes, men's and women's
societies, service clubs, laity caucuses—we have an indi-
cation of existing vehicles for the development of laity
education projects.

THE NATURE OF OUR MANDATE

Why should we worry about such matters? What is the
nature of the mandate we want to fulfill? We should be
very clear about the fact that the educational conversation
being discussed is not merely something which it would be
"nice" to initiate, nor is it to be viewed as just one more
way of working at "adult education" or "getting people
involved." The mandate is a much more serious one. It
lies at the very heart of what it means to be the church.

We have heard much in recent years about the church
as *koinonia*—"communion," "fellowship." This is an important emphasis, one that we can scarcely afford to be
without. But the church is not merely a fellowship. One
of the most dominant images in the Scriptures is that of
the *kingdom* of God. And the apostle Peter applies images
to the church which go far beyond the notion of koinonia:
"a chosen race, a royal priesthood, a holy nation, God's
own people" (1 Peter 2:9).

Each of these images deserves lengthy treatment. We
will focus here briefly on the political emphasis implicit
in references to the church as a "kingdom" or "nation."
Part of what is implied by these references is the insistence
that the church, as the gathered people of God, is itself a
corporate entity. Christians are, among other things, "sub-
jects" and "citizens" of a "kingdom" or a "nation." This is
not mere metaphor; these concepts point to very real relationships and obligations. This is why Peter immediately
goes on to remind Christians that they are "aliens and
exiles" (1 Peter 2:11).

This theme has often been distorted by Christians, especially by those who have advocated an "other-worldly" brand of Christianity. To be aliens and exiles does not mean that we ought to devalue involvement in the structures of this world. Rather, we must be involved *in* those structures as bearers of a unique "national" identity.

The mandate to function within the structures of human society as citizens of a holy nation has two important aspects, as can be seen in Peter's specific instructions to the church: "Honor all men. Love the brotherhood. Fear God. Honor the emperor" (1 Peter 2:17). Two of these directives relate to what we might think of as the *domestic policy* of the holy nation, the church. We are to fear God and love the brotherhood (and sisterhood).

The educational conversation which we have been discussing must be seen, then, as an important means of expediting this domestic policy. By talking to each other, by reading and reflecting and arguing, we are participating in the process of *realizing who we are* as the people of God. What does it mean to be a *people* who are called to be a holy nation? And what does it mean to be, not just one community among many—one of the ingredients of the melting-pot of North American society—but the very people *of God?* Our educational conversation is nothing less than a sustained attempt to answer these critical questions.

The second aspect of our mandate has to do with what we might call our *foreign policy,* as summarized in the other two directives: "Honor all men" and "honor the emperor." Our foreign policy must be contiguous with our domestic policy. There are limits, then, as to what we can do by way of honoring the State and honoring the concerns of all human beings. Each of these attempts at "honoring" must be compatible with our mandate to fear God and love the church.

These considerations also apply to the business activities of our insurance agent. Indeed, they provide us with an alternative way of formulating his concerns. When he asked how he could "bring the Lord *into* his business," he was in effect asking how his economic activity could best fulfill the mandate to fear the Lord, love the church, honor all human beings, and honor these patterns of authority which operate in his sphere of activity. In short, he was asking how his insurance business could be carried out in a way that is consistent with the domestic and foreign policy of the holy nation, the church, of which he is a citizen.

I have insisted that involvement in laity education is a means of fulfilling the domestic aspect of our Christian policy. And this, in turn, is a means of preparing ourselves for a faithful response to the demands of our foreign policy. The task of "honoring" the corporate structures of our society, while at the same time "honoring" the concerns of all human beings, is something that we must do aggressively. The holy nation, as the apostle puts it earlier in this passage, must *"declare* the wonderful deeds" of the God who has redeemed his people. The task of "declaring" cannot be carried out by words alone. It also requires that we show forth the rule of Christ over all areas of our lives, including our involvement in the corporate structures of society.

THE TASK OF THE CHRISTIAN COMMUNITY

The Christian community has not yet begun to do an effective job in this area. In recent years we have stressed the need for "fellowship" and "spirituality," and our outreach has been limited to a concern for personal evangelism and acts of charity. In many respects the task which we now face parallels the challenge posed by the need for "foreign missions" in recent centuries. Just as previous generations of Christians stressed the need for the *physical* expansion of the Christian community, "to the ends of the earth," so we must now insist on the expansion of Christian witness into all spheres of human *activity*. In this sense, our insurance agent can be viewed as a contemporary David Livingstone, standing before the "dark continent" of American business. The paths of discipleship are as yet uncharted. There is a good chance that many mistakes will be made along the way. There are legitimate reasons for a sense of fear and inadequacy.

And yet the Lord says to us, "Go into all the world"— just as he spoke these words to those who were tempted to ignore the uncharted areas of the physical world. The church of Jesus Christ—our congregations, colleges, seminaries, Bible study groups, prayer fellowships, guilds, and societies—must become a training center for this new dimension of missionary activity. Only then will we have begun to respond to our insurance agent's concerns.

Joseph Gremillion *

7.

Roman Catholic Social Teaching Since Vatican Council II

IN HIS FAREWELL SERMON DURING THE Last Supper, Jesus sums up his message and his meaning: "A new commandment I give to you, that you love one another; even as I have loved you, that you also love one another" (John 13:34).

The social teaching and social ministry of the Christian church derive primarily from this Good News that God loves us, in and through and with Christ. We become his authentic followers to the extent that we love God and each other and all the human family. "You shall love the

---

* DR. JOSEPH GREMILLION is author of *The Gospel of Peace and Justice,* a study of the documents during and after Vatican II dealing with the social teaching of the Roman Catholic Church. He is a Fellow at the University of Notre Dame, South Bend, Indiana. Father Gremillion was the former executive officer of the Pontifical Commission on Justice and Peace. He speaks several languages and has lived in Europe several years. He was also a former Parish Priest in Louisiana.

Lord your God with all your heart . . . and your neighbor as yourself" (Luke 10:27).

Serving our neighbor is the basic demand and public test of faith and of love. "Do you want to be shown, you shallow man, that faith apart from deeds is barren; . . . fulfill the royal law, according to the scripture: 'You shall love your neighbor as yourself,' . . . But if you show partiality, you commit sin, and are convicted by the law as transgressors" (James 2:20; 2:8, 9). It was the good Samaritan who helped the roadside victim despite differences of class, religion, and race, who "proved neighbor . . . 'Go, and do likewise'" (Luke 10:36–37).

Feeding the hungry, caring for the sick, concern for prisoners, provide the key evidence before Christ at the Last Judgment of all nations: "Truly, I say to you, as you did it to one of the least of these my brethren, you did it to me" (Matt. 25:40).

In Jerusalem the first Christian community, some five thousand or more went the whole way: "the company of those who believed were of one heart and soul, and no one said that any of the things which he possessed was his own, but they had everything in common. . . . distribution was made to each as any had need" (Acts 4:32–35).

Today, nineteen hundred years later, providing for the needs of all is becoming the conscious goal of economic and political life in most nations. The prime measure of a successful society and stable government is the degree to which the material and social needs of all are met in a framework of justice and human rights. Undoubtedly, the justice preached by the Hebrew prophets and the love lived by Christ and his followers provided much of the ferment to form today's vision of the just and humane society.

POPE JOHN XXIII

John XXIII served as pope for five years, 1958–63. Three actions by him are especially noteworthy in our

present context: his summoning of the Second Vatican
Council, his opening toward ecumenical and interreligious
cooperation, his two pastoral letters on economic and political affairs: *Christianity and Social Progress* and *Peace
on Earth*. (Such documents are also called "encyclicals,"
from the Greek word meaning "universal," because they
are addressed to the whole church, and even to all humankind.)

Christianity and Social Progress, in 1961, opens with
the assertion that the Church was established by Jesus
Christ so that all who enter "may find salvation as well as
the fullness of a more excellent life." Although the Church
has the special task of sanctifying souls and sharing heavenly blessings, "She is also solicitous for the requirements
of men in their daily lives, not merely those relating to
food and sustenance, but also to their comfort and ad-
vancement in various kinds of goods." (Numbers 1 and 3;
see footnote*)

Expanding the Church's concern beyond "the minimum
necessities of human life," Pope John specified that by "the
fullness of a more excellent life" he meant health services,
education, training in skills, and housing; also leisure and
recreational facilities, press, cinema, radio and television
(61). Need for "the goods and services for a better life,
. . . the advantages of a more humane way of existence,"
and for "social security," thread throughout John's teaching
(79 and 105). All of these he judged to be necessary concerns for those who would follow Christ's command to love
their neighbors as themselves. Son and brother of hard-
working peasants, John wanted this more abundant life for

---

* References to Catholic social documents are usually made by
paragraph numbers, as given above. The complete text of all
documents cited herein can be found in *The Gospel of Peace and
Justice*, Orbis Books, New York. This is a collection of the twenty-
five principal social documents issued since 1961; it is edited by
the present writer. I have also written therein an "Overview" of
150 pages, which shows the nine main developments within Catholic social teaching during the past fifteen years.

rural dwellers, too: highways, transport and marketing facilities, medical services, schools, housing, pure water supply, and "finally, furnishings and equipment needed in the modern farm home" (127).

Most significantly, John extended the concept of "neighbor" to the needy of all nations. While rejoicing grandfatherlike to see this good life reaching the homes of his Western children, John decried the widening gap between the technically advanced regions of the north and the hundred nations of the south which have but recently begun to industrialize. "The latter experience dire poverty. . . . The former enjoy the conveniences of life, . . . a sufficiency and abundance of everything" (157). This issue of global justice and development to provide for the needs and rights of all God's human family became a major subject for the Second Vatican Council.

Over a thousand bishops from the Third World brought these pastoral worries about the needs and rights of their people into St. Peter's Basilica, into the mainstream of the Church's life and ministry. They and lay leaders deplored the plight of two thousand million fellow humans, the needy and oppressed of our one fragile planet. Debate about the role of the Church for promoting justice and development, human rights, and peace went on in Vatican II for four years, 1961–65. This spread throughout our Church and greatly aroused awareness of the gospel's social dimensions and experiments in social ministry among congregations on all continents.

ON PEACE

In 1963 Pope John published his second great letter, *Peace on Earth*. It urged the building up of national and world peace through just structures which assured economic needs and political rights. John reaffirmed the traditional teaching that human rights derive from the God-given nature of each person, endowed with intelligence and free will. He stressed that the dignity of each human person—with his universal and inalienable rights—is esteemed far more highly in the light of revealed truth because: "God also created man in His own image and likeness, endowed him with intelligence and freedom, and made him lord of creation. . . . For men are redeemed by the blood of Jesus Christ. They are by grace the children and friends of God and heirs of eternal glory" (3 and 10).

But this dignity, John realized, becomes meaningful only through just institutions within the existential situation of real societies. Within most societies we find the "haves" and the "have-nots," those who possess power and those who do not. Early on, Catholic social teaching had linked the exercise of societal power and human dignity and rights to the control of productive property and to the role of government in that control. The Church never embraced capitalist views on private property, rugged individualism, and the free market as these pervaded the West during the nineteenth century. It stressed, rather, communitarian principles for the common good of all.

To understand Catholic teaching today we must go back at least to 1891 when Pope Leo XIII took the first giant step to update Catholic social teaching to face the challenge of the Industrial Revolution. His key pastoral letter addressed the new human and social problems caused by the modern factory system; its well-known Latin title, *Rerum Novarum,* means "The New Problems." In the seventy ensuing years there evolved a coherent doctrinal corpus which was splendidly expressed by John's *Christianity and Social Progress* in 1961. Therein, John has reviewed this seventy-year evolution. This shows his own level of consciousness as he began his own updating process which so marks the Catholic Church today. This evolution we will now hurriedly trace.

The 1891 letter of Leo XIII recognized that three key factors (or actors) underlie economic life: workers, productive property, and the state (that is, governmental or public authority). He showed that the just and equitable *interrelation* of these three factors, expressed corporately through institutions, is the crucial issue for Catholic social teaching in the industrial age. Pope John summarized this key relationship as given by Leo seventy years before: "Work, inasmuch as it is an expression of the human person, can by no means be regarded as a mere commodity. For the great majority of mankind, work is the only source from which the means of livelihood are drawn. Hence, its remuneration is not to be thought of in terms of merchandise, but rather according to the laws of justice and equity (18).

"Private property, including that of productive goods, is a natural right possessed by all, which the State can by no means suppress. However, as there is from nature a social aspect to private property, he who uses his right in this regard must take into account not merely his own welfare but that of others as well (19).

"The State, whose purpose is the realization of the common good in the temporal order, can by no means disregard the economic activity of its citizens. Indeed, it should be present to promote in a suitable manner the production of a sufficient supply of material goods, . . . safeguard the rights of all citizens, but especially the weaker, such as workers, women and children, . . . contribute actively to the betterment of the living conditions of workers, . . . see to it that labor agreements are entered into according to the norms of justice and equity, and that in the environment of work the dignity of the human being is not violated either in body or spirit" (20–21).

THE RIGHT TO ORGANIZE

Of primordial significance for the Church's social commitment and future ministry was Pope Leo's defense of the right of workers to organize into labor unions. In 1961 John recalled that seventy years before, ". . . in the same Letter moreover, there is affirmed the natural right of workers to enter corporately into associations, whether these be composed of workers only or of workers and management; and also the right to adopt that organizational structure judged more suitable to meet their professional needs. And the workers themselves have the right to act freely and on their own initiative within the above-mentioned associations, without hindrance and as their needs dictate" (22).

John noted approvingly that these principles have "contributed much to the establishment and promotion of that new section of legal science known as labor law," and that modern nations have adopted them into social legislation during recent decades (21). Finally, Leo's repudiation of the nineteenth century's two great contenders is recalled: "The unregulated competition" of pure capitalism, and "the class struggle in the Marxist sense, are utterly opposed to Christian teaching and also to the very nature of man" (23).

Since 1891, therefore, the Church has through its moral authority supported the role of unions for creating "worker power," which led to collective bargaining and greater participation in the economic process and product. In this way workers incorporated the only "productive property" they owned—their own time and muscle and skill, much as investors and managers had incorporated their capital and plant and skill into business enterprises. In the inevitable tension between labor and capital, government must intervene.

Pope John believed "big government" was necessary to provide for the needs and rights of all in the complex interplay of multiple dependencies among modern power groups. "Consequently, it is requested again and again of public authorities responsible for the common good, that they intervene in a wide variety of economic affairs, and that, in a more extensive and organized way than heretofore, they adapt institutions, tasks, means, and procedures to this end." He asserted for government the authority to take effective measures against mass unemployment, to keep economic fluctuations within acceptable bounds, to reduce imbalances between economic sectors, between regions within nations, and between peoples of the whole world (54).

After all this insistence on governmental action in the economic field, John reaffirmed the primary rights of private citizens: "Experience, in fact, shows that where private initiative of individuals is lacking, political tyranny prevails." Due to economic stagnation "all sorts of consumer goods and services, closely connected with needs of the body and more especially of the spirit, are in short supply. . . . Where, on the other hand, appropriate activity of the State is lacking or defective, commonwealths are apt to experience incurable disorders, and there occurs exploitation of the weak by the unscrupulous strong" (55–58).

To reconcile this constant and hopefully creative tension between individual and community, private groups and public authority, local and national and global interests, Pope John appealed to an operating method which remains central to the Church's social teaching. This is the "principle of subsidiary function" which seeks to mediate between the "bigness" of business, labor and government, on one hand, and the small groups of family, friendship, and community required for each person to become more fully human.

"It is a fundamental principle of social philosophy, fixed and unchangeable, that one should not withdraw from individuals and commit to the community what they can accomplish by their own enterprise and industry. So, too, it is an injustice and at the same time a grave evil and a disturbance of right order, to transfer to the larger and higher collectivity functions which can be performed and provided for by lesser and subordinate bodies" (53).

This *principle of subsidiarity* in the complex relations of persons and groups is popularized today under the appealing slogan, "Small is beautiful." Human social groupings at local, national, and global levels become ever more complex and in conflict with each other because of the expanding technology of industry and communications. Paradoxically, the likelihood of conflict grows because the many sectors of society become more dependent upon each other. This growing interdependence requires intervention by public authority to reconcile conflicts among groups and to promote the common good of society as a whole.

THE COMMON GOOD

In Church teaching, the *common good* is not the glib phrase of a political campaign. It forms the bedrock of Catholic social doctrine, more fundamental than government and property, because its goals and measure is the human person and his or her perfection. The common good, in Pope John's words, "embraces the sum total of those conditions of social living, whereby men are enabled more fully and more readily to achieve their own perfection."

The three criteria for the productive property (industrial production), the human investment of time and energy, and the participation of governmental structures are seen as:

(1) Contributing to the total conditions of social living (the dynamics of the economic, political, social, familial, and personal factors).

(2) Contributing to the balance between the weak, poor and oppressed, and the strong, rich and dominant.

(3) Contributing to a more vital expression of human fulfillment through a more responsible participation of all the social strata of human organizations.

To the extent and to the degree each of these institutions of society measure up to those criteria, they may be judged to be just and equitable.

Christians as individuals and as communities must love their neighbors as themselves within this changing, conflictual, and cooperating complexus of interdependencies. Above all, followers of Christ must defend the weak and oppressed against the strong and dominant. They must discern and decry injustice as did the Hebrew prophets and John the Baptist. They must foster reconciliation and forgiveness among opponents, and love for all by all, as Jesus did. They must work-with others to promote reform and just structures in society. In this way they build up the peace promised by Christ, and his kingdom.

Such is the role of social ministry—a difficult, delicate charge, a new and evolving ministry in today's technological, ever-changing national and world society. It is therefore an experimental ministry, much misunderstood even by "good Christians," especially if their wealth, position, and power are criticized, and if reforms of the *status quo* they enjoy are demanded.

Such demands by the poor and powerless have spread apace since World War II. In North America, the claims of "worker power" which marked the 1930s have been followed by the demands of "Black power," Hispanic, ethnic and Native American movements, and women's liberation.

Most nations have experienced comparable arousal of self-identity among less-favored groups who now seek full participation in the social process. On the planet as a whole, the less industrialized "have not" nations of the South have formed a Third World Forum to confront and negotiate with the technically advanced affluent West. Some nations of the Mideast, with fresh awareness of their Islamic and Arab identity, joined in 1973 with other oil-rich nations to form the Organization of Petroleum Exporting Countries (OPEC). Suddenly the "Christian West," after three centuries of global dominance over Asia and Africa, finds itself increasingly dependent upon other peoples of other cultures and faiths.

SOCIAL MINISTRY

Social ministry must address all these issues, however intertwined with economic and political institutions, however creaturely and mundane. All deal with God's creation —redeemed by Christ and destined to be made new in his kingdom when he comes again on the Last Day. Also, because through these worldly social institutions the hungry are fed, the homeless sheltered, the sick cared for, and love is expressed. And through this we are judged by Christ.

Social ministry must sometimes help the weak to overcome their own apathy, to acquire awareness of their God-given dignity and rights, to forge coalitions for reforming unjust economic and political systems. In Latin America over a hundred Catholic bishops, thousands of clergy, tens of thousands of lay leaders now focus on this ministry. They promote "conscientization" of a hundred million slum-dwellers and peasants through *communidades de base.* These are neighborhood and village groups of a score of families who reflect together on the Good News of God's love and his call to freedom and justice, who love and share and serve each other. They develop leaders who federate a dozen or a hundred groups to protest and change the unjust structures of their town and nation. Bishop Helder Camara of Brazil is their best-known leader. He espouses nonviolent methods, despite the violence used against him and associates, several of whom have been assassinated.

It is not surprising that Bishop Camara deeply admires and imitates Mahatma Gandhi, a Hindu guru, and the Rev. Martin Luther King, the Baptist preacher who has best personified social ministry within the church of the United States since the Civil War.

This social ministry for "conscientizing" oppressed groups often brings sharp criticism from conservatives within society and the Church. "Let sleeping dogs lie," becomes their urgent injunction to their pastors. That the weak would begin making demands is bad enough. That ministers would arouse and help organize them is perfidious, untraditional, and probably heretical to many "good Christians" who are economic and political conservers of the *status quo*.

HUMAN DIGNITY

Heavily stimulated by the Latin American example, by the civil rights and Chicano struggle in the United States, the peace and unity movement in Europe, and national independence in Africa and Asia, the Catholic Church has formally incorporated social ministry into its theology and universal apostolate. Vatican II solemnly expressed this in 1965 through its *Pastoral Constitution on the Church in the Modern World*. In this authoritative document the twenty-two hundred bishops of the Council built upon the Biblical method of discerning "the signs of the times," introduced by Pope John in his *Peace on Earth* in 1963. John deliberately seeks out the "distinctive characteristics" of our age which could, under Providence and in the Holy Spirit, point the way for Christian witness and ministry in the social field. Among these signs of the times John enters upon four collective and conscious demands for human dignity and rights:

1. Having begun by claiming their rights in the socioeconomic sphere, workers then make claims for full participation in political institutions and for sharing in the fields of learning and culture (40).

2. "Since women are becoming ever more conscious of their human dignity, they will not tolerate being treated as inanimate objects or mere instruments, but claim, both in domestic and in public life, the rights and duties that befit a human person" (41).

3. "Men all over the world have today—or soon will have—the rank of citizens in independent nations. No one wants to feel subject to political power located outside his own country or ethnic group. . . . On the contrary, the conviction that all men are equal by reason of their natural dignity has been generally accepted. Hence, racial discrimination can in no way be justified" (43–44).

4. Modern states organize themselves judicially through a written constitution, which includes "a charter of fundamental human rights." These practices "clearly show that the men of our time have become increasingly conscious of their dignity as human persons. This awareness prompts them to claim a share in the public administration of their country, while it also accounts for the demand that their own inalienable and inviolable rights be protected by law" (75–79).

We see here the convictions, as well as the rhetoric and headlines, which have dominated the sixties and seventies: "Humans all over the world—demanding their rights in the socioeconomic order . . . increasingly conscious of their dignity . . . a new awareness prompting them to wrest full participation in political institutions . . . women growing conscious of their due role in society." These signs of the times were evaluated in the light of the gospel by Vatican II. It decided that this discernment and 'conscientizing' of God's people should continue. Therefore, the *Pastoral Constitution on the Church in the Modern World* legislated that there be established in the central administration of the Church, in the Vatican, an office "for the worldwide promotion of justice for the poor and of Christ's kind of love for them" (90).

In January 1967, Paul VI constituted the Pontifical Commission Justice and Peace and assigned it the role of arousing all Christians to their mission of promoting justice, development, human rights, and peace within and among all nations. I was named the executive of this new department of the Vatican, where I remained until 1974. Twenty-five cardinals, bishops, religious and laity composed this top-level "ministry" of the Catholic Church. Our main task was to extend and strengthen the Church's social ministry everywhere. Some eighty national commissions were set up by bishops' conferences in all continents. Over a hundred social ministry centers now function at state and metropolitan levels in the U.S.A. All these ministries become increasingly ecumenical and interreligious.

In the spring of 1967, just as these social ministry institutes were being officially launched, Paul VI issued his pastoral letter *On the Development of Peoples*. Therein he forthrightly attacked oppressive social structures, "situations whose injustice cries to heaven," which incite grave temptation to violence. He warned that a revolutionary uprising produces new injustices and disasters. Consequently, violent revolution must be avoided—"save where there is manifest, long-standing tyranny which would do great damage to fundamental personal rights and dangerous harm to the common good of the country. . . . A real evil should not be fought against at the cost of greater misery."

A year later, in 1968, Pope Paul went to Colombia for the opening of the historic Medellin Conference of the Latin American Bishops on "The Church in the Present-Day Transformation of Latin America." Paul warmly praised the pastoral action the Church was undertaking against "systems and structures which cover up and favor grave and oppressive inequalities." Social ministry by the bishops' conferences of Bolivia, Brazil, Chile, and Mexico were specifically cited. The Medellin documents *Justice* and *Peace,* issued by this continental assembly, attacked the twofold oppression of dominant and privileged groups within each country, and "external neo-colonialism . . . international monopolies and international imperialism of money."

Liberation from this double domination and dependency was embraced as a call to ministry comparable to the call

to Moses in Exodus to free the Israelites from the bondage
of Pharaoh. From this there came forth that new doctrinal
school known as "theology of liberation." The chief pastors
of Latin America perceived the need for rapid transformation and development of their continent to be "an obvious
sign of the Spirit who leads the history of man and of
peoples toward their vocation." (*op. cit., Gospel of Peace
and Justice,* pages 18ff. and 445–476)

The political elements of social ministry were expressly
raised by Paul VI in his second substantial letter, *A Call
to Action,* in May, 1971. (The Latin title is *Octogesima
Adveniens,* because it marked the eightieth anniversary of
Pope Leo's pioneering document of 1891.) Paul returned
to "situations of injustice," both within nations and on the
global level. These have become so blatant that "many
people are reaching the point of questioning the very model
of society. . . . The need is felt to pass from economics to
politics" (45–46).

And for dealing with political power, Paul urged a
ministry by local Christian communities in ecumenical
cooperation. In view of the wide variety of economic and
political situations in different continents, cultures, and
countries, Paul did not propose solutions of universal va-
lidity. "Such is not our ambition, nor is it our mission. It
is up to the Christian communities to analyze with ob-
jectivity the situation which is proper to their own country." This insistence on the local church's role is a direct
result of Vatican II teaching on collegiality which decen-
tralizes ecclesial authority. Many new bodies now take
shape to implement this recognition of pluralism: bishops'
conferences at national and continental levels, diocesan
senates of clergy, parish councils which are in majority lay,
associations of religious, team ministries, and social witness
coalitions.

To promote interchurch cooperation in social ministry,
Pope Paul approved formation of the Committee on Society, Development and Peace, best known under the quaint

acronym *Sodepax*. This was constituted jointly by the World Council of Churches, Geneva, and the Pontifical Commission Justice and Peace, Vatican City. On an equal basis, each constituting body names members, chairpersons and staff, and provides budgetary needs. I served as Catholic co-chairman, named by Pope Paul, from 1968–75. *Sodepax* is the first ongoing institutionalized relationship between the Catholic Church and the Orthodox and Protestant churches after centuries of separation and conflict. Comparable cooperation has begun with the Jewish and Muslim communities and with the Hindu and Buddhist faiths.

In autumn 1971, 250 bishops met in the Vatican for their triennial Synod. Paul VI had assigned them the subject, "Justice in the World." The onrush of the very issues too hurriedly reviewed here, their place in preaching the gospel and in the Church's mission—in short, social ministry—received the careful corporate attention of these pastors from over a hundred nations. Their concluding document, *Justice in the World,* so succinct and striking, is now our most compelling and oft-quoted pronouncement on Catholic social teaching and social ministry. Space allows, finally, for only four paragraphs.

Gathered from the whole world, in communion with all who believe in Christ and with the entire human family, and opening our hearts to the Spirit who is making the whole of creation new, we have questioned ourselves about the mission of the People of God to further justice in the world (1).

Scrutinizing the 'signs of the times' and seeking to detect the meaning of emerging history, while at the same time sharing the aspirations and questionings of all those who want to build a more human world, we have listened to the Word of God that we might be converted to the fulfilling of the divine plan for the salvation of the world (2).

Listening to the cry of those who suffer violence and are oppressed by unjust systems and structures, and hearing the

appeal of a world that by its perversity contradicts the plan
of its Creator, we have shared our awareness of the Church's
vocation to be present in the heart of the world by proclaiming
the Good News to the poor, freedom to the oppressed, and
joy to the afflicted (5).

Action on behalf of justice and participation in the transformation of the world fully appear to us as a constitutive
dimension of the preaching of the Gospel, or, in other words,
of the Church's mission for the redemption of the human race
and its liberation from every oppressive situation (6).

Examples of
Corporate Witness

*Leon Jaworski ***

8.

Moral Foundations of Government

I WANT TO SPEAK TO YOU IN THIS CHAPTER about foundations—foundations that make a state strong and a nation great. I want to lay aside, if only for these few minutes, the concerns and the fears that you and I share about taxes, the energy problem, the rising inflation, and other clouds of concern that stem from economic woes. I want to ask you to think with me about moral foundations in representative government.

Nothing captivates me more than a good sermon, and every now and then I hear what I would term a great sermon. I have heard them in my city and in this city. I heard such a sermon when I was on duty in Washington. The pastor of the First Presbyterian Church in Philadelphia

---

* LEON JAWORSKI served as Special Prosecutor in the Watergate case and is currently serving in the same capacity in the "Korea-gate" investigation.

This is an address he delivered to the Austin Area Conference of Churches on Sunday, January 30, 1977, in the First Methodist Church, Austin, Texas, honoring the members of the Texas Legislature. The address is exactly as delivered, with the exception of the first paragraph which was omitted with permission of Mr. Jaworski.

was filling the pulpit in the New York Avenue Presbyterian Church in Washington. His sermon was on the subject of seeking a city, taking his text from Hebrews 11:10, "For he looked for a city which hath foundations, whose builder and maker is God." It was Abraham who was seeking such a city and, when, in his sermon, this illustrious preacher laid out the elements of a city "which hath foundations," he said: "Seek the law, seek the word. Seek to do good. The old truth remains, you see, that you cannot achieve good by evil means. Apparently nothing is so difficult to understand in our present society. The tired old excuse is still that the end justifies the means. It has always been wrong. It is wrong still."

What this great minister was driving home is the word from Holy Writ that there is no way either a nation, or a state, or a community, if you please, can blossom and flourish into greatness unless it has foundations of truth and integrity.

Nicholas Murray Butler was a great American who not only served as President of Columbia University but also answered the call of our government in numerous post-World War I international peace conferences. Fifty-six years ago, he delivered an address on "The Changing Foundations of Government." He referred to the startling changes that were taking place at the "very foundations of our political and economic life." He remarked that the "foundations of American government and of American life are being moved, and it is of high importance that we should understand what is moving them and whither they are moving." He added: "Only then shall we be able to determine whether the movement is for good or for ill."

At the time of this soul-searching address, Nicholas Murray Butler was deeply concerned that the "movement" was not "for good but for ill."

I wish that it were possible for me to give you more of his comments, but a few of these chosen excerpts will suffice to illustrate what preyed on his mind. He said: "The

precepts of liberty and the dictates of justice, as these have
been through the long history of human progress, are
treated lightly and unconcernedly when they appear to
stand in the way of some immediate interest, some individual ambition or some group privilege. Yet it was precisely to these ends that those principles and those dictates
were brought into existence at such stupendous cost of
human experience. . . . It is through lack of knowledge
of the history and meaning of the underlying principles of
government and through lack of foresight as to what will
happen if those principles are put aside or overthrown that
men and political parties and legislatures and courts march
so jauntily toward the achievement of some immediate
purpose which affects the interests or stirs the emotions of
men."

Next Butler spoke of "the steadily growing incapacity of
representative government and the steadily increasing lack
of confidence in it; of the unwillingness to subordinate an
immediate advantage to a future gain; of the dissatisfaction
with any principle or rule of conduct, however noble or
however hoary with age and honorable with service, that
stands in the way of individual or group interests."

One of his conclusions was as follows: "We need quickly
to strengthen the foundations of representative government
and thereby rebuild public confidence in it. This can only
be done by attracting to the political service of the state
men and women of the highest type of intelligence and
character, *who have no personal or group ends to serve.*"

Well, this was fifty-six years ago. Has anything come to
our attention in recent years that makes Dr. Butler's words
prophetic? Was he an alarmist or was he a seer?

Let me direct your attention to the Report of the Watergate Special Prosecution Force, released recently. I did
not write this Report, although much of what it contains is
based on matters that came to light while I served as Special
Prosecutor. But members of the staff, who saw what I saw
and came to know what I had learned, wrapped up in these

words what had occurred during what may be termed as the Watergate era—and some of which occurred even prior thereto. Here is what the Report says, and this part I fully approbate:

In considering what recommendations to include in this Report, WSPF concentrated on what it did observe: criminal abuse of power by government officials in high places; . . . unchallenged, subjective judgments by the executive branch in identifying persons and organizations that constitute an impermissible threat to the national interest and to executive policy; an undemocratic condition wherein money is power, and skillful, cynical public relations cements that power; and finally, a silent, sometimes grudging, sometimes willful conclusion by some government representatives that ethical standards are irrelevant because quick implementation of policy goals is mandatory, but achievable only by social and personal injustices to others.

Let us all remember that Watergate, in its broad sense, did not begin with the breakin. It took root and began to grow step by step decades ago. Let me share with you this paragraph contained in the Special Prosecutor's Report:

Many of the Watergate phenomena had their historical precedents. Many had grown with no deterrence from other branches of government. Others had grown without questions from the people and the press.

Well, as the Watergate report points out, some of the wrongs and excesses of which it speaks did not begin with the so-called Watergate era. They escalated to unprecedented heights during that era. If there be those whose attitude is one of indifference to these disclosures—who dismiss it with a shrug of the shoulders and with the comment, "So what—it has been going on for a long time," let me point out to them that more than one nation in history has met with disaster by just such an apathy of its people.

It is apropos, I believe, to bring to your attention two writings, about 150 years apart.

In 1831 there was a young man from France, only twenty-six years of age, but already accomplished in scholarship, philosophy, and statesmanship, who was sent by the French government to our country primarily to examine prisons and penitentiaries. He became intrigued by our system of government and its institutions and therefore devoted considerable time to analyzing life in America. On his return, he wrote his classic *Democracy in America,* published in 1835 and again in 1840. This volume represented a wide-ranging study of the political and social institutions of the United States. Scholars have commented that the result of de Tocqueville's visit to America, and the writings that followed, brought forth not only "the greatest book ever written in America but probably the greatest on any national polity and culture."

In summarizing what he found in our country, he said:

> I sought for the greatness and genius of America in her commodious harbors and her ample rivers, and it was not there;
> I sought for the greatness and genius of America in her fertile fields and boundless forests, and it was not there;
> I sought for the greatness and genius of America in her rich mines and her vast world commerce, and it was not there;
> I sought for the greatness and genius of America in her public school system and her institutions of learning, and it was not there;
> I sought for the greatness and genius of America in her democratic Congress and her matchless Constitution, and it was not there.

Then, after he paid tribute to the pulpits that were "aflame with righteousness," in ringing words he declared: "America is great because America is good, and if America ever ceases to be good, America will cease to be great."

Almost a century and one-half later, there came to my desk a letter typical of countless similar communications I have received during the past two years. It was written by a student in government who resides in Madison, Wisconsin. The pertinent parts of this letter read as follows:

I have majored in political science and history and have always thought of doing good for my nation.

Each day new revelations come out on how corrupt men have made our government. I feel as if I have a complete void in my heart where the feeling of patriotism is to be.

This is why I am writing to you. Please, would you tell me how I can regain trust in my elected officials?

What is important to remember, and what I want to reiterate, is that this does not constitute the isolated view of a disquieted student. To so believe is to stick one's head in the sand, because this identical concern, voiced in different ways, is deeply rooted among many young people across our land from shore to shore. I have concrete evidence of it.

A large number of young Americans have written to me —a goodly number have spoken to me—about the moral and ethical values of public officials. These standards and principles of conduct have taken on an added dimension in their outlook of judging leadership at all levels of government. Good, reliable, trustworthy leadership will gain their regard and support. A lack of moral foundations, the absence of probity and trust, will turn them away.

It is basic that the older generation, as well as the younger generation, as good citizens must concern themselves, and deeply, with the problems of government, both international and domestic, with peace, with economic soundness, and with social gains. But this is not enough— more is needed. As these challenges are faced, we must ever hold before us the pronouncement of Thomas Jefferson at the time he was drafting the Declaration of Independence: "The whole art of government," he said, "consists in the art of being honest." And if you consider this comment to be an oversimplification of the art of government, then let me express to you my firm belief that

Jefferson's premise at least must serve as the foundation of government, and if the honesty of which he speaks is absent, sooner or later the affairs of government are sure to fail.

We seem to be discussing a very timely topic. Note with me, if you please, the comments on the editor's page of *U. S. News & World Report,* written about a year ago.

If moral education is about to make a comeback, there are those who are convinced it is just in the nick of time. They trace rising crime, political chicanery, even inflation, the federal deficit and setbacks in foreign policy to a nationwide decline in moral and ethical values that have been eroding at an accelerated pace for years.

The world is littered with the ruins of societies destroyed by irresponsibility. We cannot succeed by trying to treat the symptoms—crime, anger, hostility, poverty and war. We must seek the root causes and deal with them.

Any signal of increasing interest in the study of morals and ethics can be taken as an indicator that today's young people do, indeed, care about such things.

Prime Minister Disraeli told us that the youth of a nation are the trustees of posterity. This admonition is easy to understand and to accept. If we embrace this truism and give it proper regard, it follows that the youth of our nation are our society's most precious possession. If they are to become disenchanted with our institutions of government —then posterity will not be served by fiduciaries of confidence and faith and trust in our democratic concepts. Rather posterity then will be served by trustees of disenchantment and indifference, leading perhaps to radical changes from a system which, fundamentally, today is unexcelled.

Last year, I stood in the hallowed room in Independence Hall in Philadelphia where the Declaration of Independence was signed and eleven years later, after four months of debate, deliberation, study, and prayer, our Constitution was drafted. There were vast differences of opinions and a great contrariety of views permeating these extensive sessions on the Constitution, yet in the end dissents were largely resolved by an understanding approach to opposing views of the participants and the acceptance of sincereness and good faith on the part of all. The eventual result was a monumental document that has stood the test of time and has enabled us daily to enjoy the freedoms and the individual rights it guarantees.

As I contemplated the setting in Independence Hall, as it existed almost two hundred years ago, there crossed my mind, more deeply than ever before, the hardships, the sacrifice, and above all else, the selflessness of these great patriots who gave so much to earn for generations to come the freedoms that are ours today. They risked being captured, regarded as traitors, and being put to death. And as I walked away from this historic place, there returned afresh the eloquent expressions of dedication and devotion that meant so much to them and which they hoped would be as fervently embraced by us. To remind me—almost to haunt me—came the recollections of immortal words they penned—"that all men are created equal"—"life, liberty and the pursuit of happiness"—and, finally, the pledge to each other of "our lives, our fortunes and our sacred honor." Then I paused to wonder: are these just empty phrases to many of us today, or are they still as radiant, as inspirational, and as binding in our pursuits as they were to these great founders of freedom and seekers of justice? I could not stop with these musings. What tortured my thinking was the undivided and unquestioned integrity and probity of these patriots—their trustworthiness and guilelessness—as contrasted with the shams and deceits and corruptions perpetrated by some of their successors of modern times.

What were the characteristics of the Founders who gave birth to this nation? And of the framers who cast our Constitution? Were they self-serving and greedy? Or were they men and women who loved freedom and justice and placed on the altar of sacrifice their fortunes—even their lives—to attain these ends? We gain some semblance of understanding of what plagues us today when we compare their sacrificial dedication to the conduct of some of our people in government today. But as we deplore their disgraceful conduct, let us applaud and never forget the exemplary and dedicated labors of so many of the public servants in our State, in the Legislature, and elsewhere.

Still fresh on my mind is the sadness of seeing one of the great tragedies of modern history—men who once had fame in their hands sinking to infamy—all because eventually their goals were of the wrong dreams and aspirations. The teaching of right and wrong had been forgotten and little evils were permitted to grow into great evils—small sins to escalate into big sins. How did Alexander Pope put it? "Unblemished, let me live or die unknown. Give me an honest fame or give me none."

The Founders of this nation would have been shocked at the Watergate revelations. Then they would have concluded that despite the failures, shortcomings, and wrongdoings on the Washington scene, they still had faith and optimism in the determination and dedication of this and future generations to carry forth the spirit of America and to attain the American ideal.

When I pause to contemplate the evil of tampering with the administration of justice, of obstructing it and prostituting it, I think of Saint Thomas More who breathed life into one of the greatest of all obligations of man—that of unswerving loyalty to the ends of justice. Not justice for the affluent and the powerful alone, not justice for the admired and the favored alone, not justice alone for those whose views and beliefs are shared, but justice as well for the weak, for the poor, and even for the despised and the scorned.

St. Thomas More is best known in history for his courageous and sacrificial resistance of the evil demands of his King, whom he served as Lord Chancellor. He placed his conscience above life itself. It has been aptly said that he "reverenced the goodness of authority but reverenced even more the authority of goodness." Do you recall his last words on the scaffold? "I die the King's good servant, but God's first."

In eloquent terms and with lustrous integrity, this great man in history made his point in clear and unmistakable terms: you do not follow an obviously corrupt and evil leader.

Nothing leaves me with such a lack of faith and confidence in aspirants to public office and spokesmen of political parties than to hear them wail about some of the problems of today, without saying one word of the need of foundations of truth, justice, and honor in public affairs. The question naturally arises: do they just assume them to be there, or do they even care?

In my own home state, I was saddened to read the appeal of a man interested in his own political future. He was urging his listeners to elect three men to Congress belonging to a certain political party. He did not consider it necessary for them to have any other qualifications than to be a member of that particular party. Whether they were men of honor and trust seemed to be beside the point. What was important to him was having three bodies voting the straight party line. This is precisely what America does not need.

There was an English statesman named Shaftesbury— perhaps you never heard of him—who spoke words that should be embraced by us all and never forsaken by those who serve in government. He put it thusly: "The most natural beauty in the world is honesty and moral truth."

I always admired Henry L. Stimson, a great public servant, who inspired confidence in his devoted service. It was he who said that "The sinfulness and weakness of man are evident to anyone who lives in the active world. But men are also great, kind and wise. Honor begets honor;

trust begets trust; faith begets faith; and hope is the main-spring of life."

Public officials face many trials and tribulations—many face great temptations. When they have come to grips with their responsibilities and have dealt with the issues inherent in their duty to God and to fellowman, let us hope that they can say, as did Abraham Lincoln at the end of the Civil War: "I have felt His hand upon me in great trials."

I would add these thoughts. Shortcomings and failures notwithstanding, we should be proud of America and evidence that pride with acclaim and enthusiasm. There is no other country like ours in the entire world. We can and must keep America great, not only for ourselves, but as well for the leadership our nation gives to the rest of the world, and we have as much, if not more, reason to point with pride to our own State. Texas still has problems to overcome—it always will—but Texas has not turned its back on social and moral values that must be faced and then embraced.

I leave you with these thoughts, and let us hope and pray that our nation and our State will always have foundations whose builder and maker is God.

Donald W. Shriver, Jr. *

9.

From Jerusalem to Nashville: Urban Mission for Southern Christians

NOTHING IS MORE CHARACTERISTIC OF US southerners than for us to introduce each other with the question, "Where are you *from?*" The answer for me has to be in terms of cities. My life is a tale of nine cities, the places, mostly southern, where I have lived for one or more years: Norfolk, Charlotte-Davidson, Richmond, New Haven, Gastonia, Boston, Raleigh, Atlanta, and New York. As a string of cities, the list is enough to tag me for what I

---

* DR. DONALD W. SHRIVER, JR. is President, Union Theological Seminary in New York City. He delivered this address to the 117th General Assembly of the Presbyterian Church in the United States in Nashville, Tennessee, on June 19, 1977. While specific references are made throughout to the Presbyterian Church, U.S., and to the south, in the Editor's opinion these references can be extended to all the churches and to the entire country with a little "sanctified imagination." Since the address is concerned with the corporate city as such, the theme of this book, the laity at work in the world, is well illuminated by Dr. Shriver's penetrating remarks.

am: a city boy, born in a city, educated in cities, serving
as a minister of the Presbysterian church for twenty years
in cities, and living now in what some would call the greatest, the biggest, the best, or the worst city of them all.

Why would anyone consent to have his life told in a
tale of that many cities? It may sound pretentious to say
so, but the reason grows out of all that Christians ought to
mean by the doctrine of God's calling. When all the jokes
about higher salary and prestige have been told, Presbyterian ministers go and come on the face of the earth because, in one deep sense or another, God calls us hither
and thither. At our best we try to imitate the apostle who
learned to obey a heavenly vision on the road from Jerusalem to Damascus and who learned to interrupt his jour-
neys in Asia in response to a call from Macedonia. We tag
his missionary career, like the letters he wrote, by the
names of cities. And his ambition to "preach the gospel in
Rome also" we understand as one step in a long line of
apostles, bishops, and reformers who named their vocations,
their times, and their niches in church history by cities as
diverse as Hippo, Paris, Geneva, Edinburgh, Boston, and
Nashville.

THE CITIES OUR HANDS HAVE MADE

Our urban ambivalence has two roots: one is only two
or three centuries old. Thornton Wilder was speaking of
those several centuries when he said that for the southerner,
"Place, environment, relations, repetitions, are the breath
of their being." We are a people proud of *dirt:* rich black
dirt in the coastal plain; red, stubborn dirt in the Piedmont;
even rocky dirt in the mountains. The "old place" is forever home for us, a place not defined as a mere lot in a
city. We like our crossroads grocery stores, our small towns
where everyone knows everyone else. Our roots, we say,
are in a family whose members "come home" once a year
for dinner on the grounds. We see ourselves proudly as the

last provincials, bound together by an amalgam of places, communities, families, and relations that all add up to a "culture." Deep in the most recent century of that culture is a great historical tragedy, compounded of a "peculiar institution" of which our white forebears were secretly ashamed and which our black forebears as secretly despised, compounded also of a defeat in war more disastrous than that suffered by any other region of this country. We are the most history-minded of regional peoples. We *have* to remember history: it *hurt* so much. We have to keep on remembering it until its hurt has been removed.

Add all this up, of course, and you get a culture often called "conservative." It is also, on the face of it, a culture not much urban. How very contrary is urban culture besides all these southern things: instead of dirt, concrete and steel; instead of fixed places, unending mobility of buying and selling, new "positions" and "transfers"; instead of small, intimate crossroads communities, ever-expanding conglomerates of populations who come from all corners of the earth; instead of families whose members touch each other's lives all their lives long, children who may seek their fortunes in four cities on two continents. Instead of repetitions and uniformities of custom and behavior, unending innovation: no landscape or human life unsubject to change. Instead of respect for history, reaching out and up for the future; instead of sober respect for the sufferings, "the thousand natural shocks that flesh and blood are heir to," a culture that values science as the cure to pain, truth as bendable into technology, persons as producers, communities as profit centers, and cities as competitors in growth.

You could take off from this into an account of all the reasons southerners have amassed in their literature for their deep ambivalence toward the life and culture of cities. Hardly a southern writer fails to talk about it. Willie Morris, newly arrived in New York from Mississippi and Texas, could put his feeling about the "big city" in a paragraph

that has been written many times by many of us in one
form or another:

> For in the city after a while, one got inured to the callous-
> ness, the senseless violence, the lack of simple courtesy every-
> where, for these became a part of the very fabric of one's life.
> The provincial could even become inured, after a fashion, to
> the terrible claustrophobia . . . the isolation of living on the
> same hall or in the same building for years without knowing
> the names of his neighbors and fellow apartment-dwellers. All
> I knew about the man who lived a few feet across the hall
> from my apartment was that he had a stereo, liked Bach, and
> subscribed to the *Saturday Review*. The positive aspect of this
> isolation was, of course, privacy, for in the city, indoors at
> least, one had the inalienable right to be left alone, free of the
> petty inquisitiveness, the totalitarian moralities, of the Ameri-
> can small town. (*North Toward Home,*[1] p. 370–71.)

A CITY NOT MADE WITH HANDS?

Yet that is not all, and that is not enough to explain our
ambivalence toward city life. We have a root for some of
these things approximately *thirty-three* centuries deep. Like
many of you I was impressed by the television version of
Alex Haley's *Roots;* but there was a dimension of black
American history missing in that dramatic series: the root-
age of the American black historical imagination, not only
in tribal central Africa, but in tribal northeastern Africa: I
mean the tribes of Israel. It is not true that black and white
Christians meet each other historically only in a plantation
culture. More profoundly, we meet each other in the wilderness of Sinai, around the fleshpots of Egypt, where Israel
toiled in slavery to build the great store-cities of Pharaoh
. . . and *that* is where our forefathers and foremothers
learned first to hate cities. That is where they first determined to become "wandering Aramaeans," to seek a better
country, a better city, whose builder and maker is the Lord
"who brought us up out of Egypt."
    It is no secret how, down through a thousand years of

scriptural narrative, the prophets, the apostles, the anointed One of Israel himself look at cities through mingled hope and tears. Bethel, Samaria, Nineveh, Babylon, Rome, *even* Jerusalem: what are they but places of idolatrous greed, power, and exploitations? Who would ever confuse the City of God with *these* cities? No Hebrew, no Christian in his or her right mind. But neither would any confuse the farms of Tekoa, the crossroad town of Nazareth, or the "model city" of Philippi with the kingdom of God, either.

Therefore we are a people with "no continuing city." We do not expect to be comfortably at home in any place yet invented by human cultures. We have our quarrels with them all, for we are sons and daughters of the prophets; we have our message for them all, for we are sons and daughters of the apostles; and we have our hope for the redemption of them all, for we are disciples of him who emptied himself, taking the form of a servant, pouring out his life for us outside a city wall, to break down forever the walls that divide us all from God and from our neighbors of all times and places.

Now that's telescoping a lot of theology. It's just a suggestion of why, in Biblical and Christian faith, we *have* to be ambivalent about urbanization. It's a signal sent up to remind all of us Christians that our suspicions of city life have deeper roots than merely southern history. We may dream of an "alabaster city gleaming undimmed by human tears," but it's not because we once paid a visit to Atlanta! The Lord has something better than Atlanta in mind for his people.

What? Urban Christians should have an answer. Hoping to contribute to an answer, I hasten from scripture and history toward issues that seem to emerge for us who live and move and have our contemporary Christian being in the cities of the south and the north and the east and the west of this waning twentieth century A.D. Where is the God of Israel, the God and Father of our Lord Jesus Christ,

leading his urbanizing pilgrim people these days? It's a set
of fallible perspectives, but I offer three for your consideration:

A. *Cities in the south have begun to acquire reputations
as centers of wealth, power, and prestige, at a moment in
history when God seems to be moving against the rich, the
powerful, and the proud. What word of judgment must the
southern church speak in the midst of such cities?*

Martin Luther King, Jr., used to say that the best description of the modern southerner was an old confession:
"I ain't what I oughta be, I ain't what I'm gonna be, but I
ain't what I was." In recent years, even months, we southerners have begun to gloat about it. *We* have a president
now. At last, a U.S. president with no detectable accent!
We even have a new regional name: the Sunbelt, a phrase
that images for us all the social-economic-political reality
behind the statement of a Texas congressman to a meeting
in Alabama a year ago: "The population, the wealth and
the power are moving our way now." For a generation
they have been moving our way in the form of oil rigs,
banking investment, corporate headquarters, shiny sky-
scrapers, and suburban housing spread out across the roll-
ing Piedmont like whitecaps on the endless sea of abundant
land.

We're proud of all that. Like H. Brandt Ayers of Annis-
ton, Alabama, we have lived so long under the *scorn* of
Americans who were richer, better educated, and allegedly
smarter than southerners, that we rejoice to the point of
glee over the things that are coming our way now. One
sure sign of the glee is the editorial comment in newspapers
across the south over the troubles of northern cities like
the one I now live in. It is a weird experience to shift from
a southern to a northern city in the very year (1975) when
leaders of southern cities began to chorus their superiority
to leaders of northern cities. "How are the mighty fallen!"
Why, the prophet Nahum did not rejoice more gleefully
over the fall of Nineveh than leaders in Dallas and Atlanta

have been rejoicing over the near-fall of New York City. How humanly understandable it all is: I was crossing the corner of Fifth Avenue and 59th Street the other day, passing right under the great gilded statue of William Tecumseh Sherman. *You waster of Israel,* I said to myself. *You burner of meek villages like Atlanta and Columbia. Now you stand beside a park that New York's budget can hardly keep in green grass, not to speak of summertime Shakespeare.*

It was the *mean* side of this particular recent resident of Atlanta coming out. It was the unconverted side of this particular Christian. Dr. Rachel Henderlite used to talk about the "resurrection of one area of our life after another," and this is one such area in me. A couple of years ago I asked a Sunday school class in Atlanta if they believed in the forgiveness of sins. "Sure," they said. "Then isn't it about time that we forgave General Sherman for burning down this city?" "No!" they chorused with spontaneous merriment. "Never!" Well, it may be a bit of harmless ceremony even to ask the question; but it is a serious matter to reflect that, before you can forgive anyone's sins against you, you must first identify the sin and vow yourself not to imitate it. On neither count, to my mind, has the contemporary urban American south done its moral-theological homework, nor have the churches of the south helped enough yet in that homework. The great theme of postbellum southern history has been, "If you can't lick 'em, join 'em." Writing from Nashville, John Egerton put it down in a recent issue of the *New York Times*. The trouble with the New South, he said, is that

it looks suspiciously like the Old North warmed over. . . . We have made great strides in eliminating racism—but the disease is still in us, buried deep, discreetly masked in code words such as "massive busing" and "reverse discrimination." We have built glittering new cities of glass and steel—but they look like the cities of the North, and they empty at night as streams of cars retreat to Scarsdales beyond our moated freeways. . . .

We have supplemented our agricultural economy with modern industry, and in the process have made farming impossible for all but the corporate giants of agribusiness. We have sought and welcomed Northern industrial wealth—even in those instances when they led to air and water pollution, absentee ownership, and exploitation of nonunion labor. . . .

(It all) strikes me as a terrible price to pay for readmission to the Union. Without longing nostalgically for the mythical "good old days" of the old South, I lament the steady erosion of the region's best qualities. For all of its flaws, the South has had a sense of history, of grace and space, of soul. . . . The crowning irony (is): Having a Southerner in the White House, far from slowing the pace of assimilation, may actually hasten the process.[2]

The key terms in such a critique, obviously, are moral, even theological: our "best qualities . . . grace . . . soul." What *are* the best qualities of human life . . . in cities and everywhere else? Christians, when they think social ethics, have some answers to that question. The Hebrews did also. President Carter quoted one of the Bible's great shorthand answers to the ethical question in his inauguration: "What does the Lord require of you but to do justice, to love mercy, and to walk humbly with your God?" (Micah 6:8) Southern urban churches must learn to interpret that text to their urban environments, if necessary in terms of painful judgment upon our corporate sins.

To do justice:

Done so much injustice over the years, southerners black and white have a lot to remember about the miseries of urban exploitation: The Yankee traders who, to the horror of their Puritan predecessors, turned commerce into their religion, trading anything from any place for money. The textile mill investors who connived with poor white Appalachians to be sure that manufacturing would be an occupation for white folk only. The freight-rate-setters of a Republican Congress, who made sure that the south continued for a postwar generation to supply many raw materials and few manufactures to Pittsburgh, Chicago, and New York. Not much justice in all this. Our brothers and sisters in the north admit it now, the best of them do. And the best of us will not consent to any more doing of such injustice. Yet the farmers of southern Georgia still have the sense that in its postwar incarnation the city of Atlanta is the source of many a trouble in rural Georgia; for the land deals, the loans, the search for nonunion labor, get *organized* and *financed* in Atlanta; and what the northern city once did to the rural south now gets done on another scale in another homegrown southern city. Will the church study, proclaim, and help to achieve a different relation between riches and poverty than this "burden of southern history" might teach us to imitate?

To love mercy:

Surely one of the ancient characteristics of urbanism is the vigorous development of a money economy, which tends to be merciless. In eighth century Israel, money was a traumatic development that staggered the imagination of the Elijahs and the Amoses of the land. "They sell the needy for a pair of shoes" (Amos 2:6). Have you ever had the experience, or the nightmare, of being in a large city without a dime in your pocket? In our civilization, money talks. The whisper of mercy is hard to hear in downtown Memphis.

One of the cruelties of the current urban budget crunch in New York City is the cutback in some of the human services that were originally designed to make the city a place where the poor have maximum chance to improve themselves. The City University, for instance: the largest tuition-free university system in the United States, the one chance that some residents of Harlem and the South Bronx have for getting a college education. It was a mercy, wasn't it? Or was it a "welfare boondoggle for freeloaders"? Watch what you name it, for you bear the name of Jesus, and you are not permitted as his disciples to go around naming people and systems by names coined in the lounge of the

country club. The city of God, far off though it may be, is
a place where people love mercy more than money! Put
their money to work for mercy's sake. It's a standard for
the church's prophetic criticism of how things are organized
in every city of this land.

To walk humbly with God:

Pride may be an understandable human characteristic,
but individually and corporately, it's a vice for Christians.
In the Atlanta airport you can still see an advertisement
with a big bulldozer in it: "Atlanta, City Without Limits."
If you want the theological counter to that, check the Book
of Revelation, which deals with Rome and every other
proud human construction whose architects will not acknowledge their human limits. Atlanta has limits all right;
the only question is how its people will discover them. Will
they look fifteen years into the future and calculate how
many gallons of water the Lord sends down upon the
mountains and into the Chattahoochee River? Will they
plan the limits of their urban growth accordingly? *Without
limits!* The only agent in the universe to whom Christians
are permitted by their creed to ascribe *that* characteristic
is the great God Almighty! For the rest, it is humility before him and under him.

We verge here, of course, on an ancient problem of the
churches in the south. As a region we have often been so
much under the gun of criticism from people outside that
we did not have much heart for criticizing ourselves. As
C. Vann Woodward put it, whatever reservations the
south's critics have had about our virtues, they have not
been reluctant conceding to us our vices. Well, it is time
for southern Christians to identify, to concede, perhaps to
forgive, but also to fight against, our vices. Which means
that we cannot be celebrators of cities that permit the few
to become rich overnight from real estate speculation that
locks the middle class into paying high mortgages for the
next forty years. Nor can we celebrate cities that organize

themselves chiefly around shopping centers and freeways
because commerce is the ultimate concern of those who
serve on the city council.

Will there be a word of accurate, humanizing *judgment*
leveled from the churches of southern cities on such things?
Time will tell; Christians—the salt of even the urban earth
—will tell, if they are faithful.

B. *The southern city has entered the national stage at a
moment in world history when God seems intent on testing
the human race's capacity to live as a global community.
What will the church do to enhance that capacity?*

Historian Sam Bass Warner says that nothing has been
a more powerful force as shaper of American cities in the
mid-twentieth century than the Federal Government's commitments of money for the building of highways, airports,
and defense plants.[3] Modern Los Angeles, Dallas, Atlanta,
and Jacksonville are unimaginable without the combination
of at least two out of these three. No one in the Sun Belt
seriously wants to secede from the Union anymore, because
the economic ties of our major cities with other major cities
are now multitudinous and inescapable. If "no man is an
island," as John Donne said, no city is an island anymore
either. The walled medieval city went out of fashion with
gunpowder, and the isolated American city went out of
fashion with the completion of the Erie Canal and railroads.
True enough, in our suburban retreats many of us dwell
momentarily upon the pleasures of isolation from the grime
and crime of the central city. And one has instinctive
sympathy with Willie Morris when he says that he wishes
"John Donne could have taken the Seventh Avenue (Subway) during the morning rush hour, before sitting down to
write about islands, clods, promontories, bells." [4] Too many
bells in the city toll for me already! But alas, the number
of bells is increasing, some adding to the clamor of modern
life, some faintly promising the arrival of some new music
in the world.

Some of the music is the song of a global human community. And here the modern city and the modern Christian church have a rendezvous with each other. Twenty years ago in Gastonia, North Carolina, Peggy and I noticed that the local newspaper was rather thin in its coverage of international news. One of the most frequently noted international events in that newspaper, in fact, was a churchly event: the visit of a *missionary* from Africa, Asia, or Latin America. I have no doubt that for many southern Christians the sense of reality about "foreign lands" has come in two sorts of experiences: war and the missionary movement. The Southern Presbyterian Church was born on a crest of the nineteenth century missionary movement. We have always been proud that we "unfurled our banners to the world" with Matthew 28:19 written on the banners. Always southern *agriculture* has its international dimensions; what were slavery and the cotton market if not international? And southern religion (so inferior to the northerners did it feel after the war) had no nerve for sending missionaries to New York and Chicago. Instead, we sent our missionaries to the Congo, China, and Brazil.

Now Congo, China, and Brazil are coming back to us. They are coming back into our cities as students, new employees, or jobseekers. More massively and impersonally they are coming in the form of competitors in the manufacturing market and rivals for resources like oil which we need to complete our own industrialization. Ironically enough, they are coming in the form of investments that make us newly dependent upon the decisions of governments as far away as Saudi Arabia and South Africa. Fifty million Middle Eastern oil dollars are invested in one hotel in Atlanta. Corporations with headquarters in Houston, Miami, and Raleigh-Durham are performing contracts with Middle Eastern countries, building oil derricks in the Persian Gulf, new housing in Tehran, and highways in Tanzania. (One of the surprises of my life as a traveler was going down a dirt road outside of Dar es Salaam in Tanzania, and noting the road-builder sign: "Nello Teer, Durham, North Carolina, U.S.A.") While a North Carolinian was building a road for the socialist Tanzanians, the Communist Chinese were building a railroad not far away. It is an image of the intersection of all the sections of an urban global civilization.

And what must the church do, say, and be in such a new civilization under the sun? It is difficult to know, but we had better begin with an image of ourselves akin to that portrayed in the second chapter of the Book of Acts: men and women of all nations assembled under one roof and taught by the Spirit who raised Jesus to understand each other's diverse languages. But that brings us to the threat and the promise of a reality that goes by the name of "pluralism."

THE PROBLEM OF PLURALISM

In a strange way, urban culture both threatens and promises the universalism of the human community. By no coincidence did the Christian church have its birthday in that season of the Jewish year when "men from every nation under heaven" were most likely to be present in Jerusalem, the city of peace (Acts 2:5). Our modern name for it is pluralism, which might be defined as the readiness of people to live together in society while living out of very different values, faiths, and interpretations of life. Modern people stream into cities to enjoy the elixir of "privacy," the right to be a unique individual among other unique individuals. Almost paradoxically, the big crowds of city life spawn individualism. In a New York west side Presbyterian church, where my family attends, no Sunday passes without the congregation including representatives of five or six countries, and a multitude of personal differences bridged by the name of Jesus. I have no doubt that the fruits of the nineteenth century missionary movement in Africa, Latin America, and Asia are present every Sunday in that church. More powerfully and poignantly present is the hunger of urbanized individuals for touch with each other and with the organizing center of their lives. Whatever else the urban church has to offer to the world of the pluralistic city, it has the message that nothing in even the urban world can separate the least of human beings from One whose love will not let us go.

The urban church is surrounded by people only too willing to let each other go, but the church defines itself as a fellowship of people whose loyalty to each other audaciously reflects the loyalty of Jesus Christ. Ever and again, my life as a resident of upper Broadway gets haunted by my memory of a movie, *The Pawnbroker,* which starred Rod Steiger. The issue of that movie is ancient in human affairs: is there anywhere an unconditional love? For any Jewish survivor of the Nazi concentration camps, like the pawnbroker, the question well deserves a cynical answer. The movie, you may remember, ends with the fantastic answer of a young Spanish man who decided to echo the word and deed of One who said, "Greater love has no man than this, that he lay down his life for his friend."

THE ANSWER OF INCARNATE LOVE

The preaching of the gospel in the midst of the thousand, loveless idols of modern cities demands a lot of *enacted* love. It demands an unceasing attempt to demonstrate in action, against much contrary evidence, that somebody's love can be counted on in this world, unconditionally, without price, without fail. The best we Christians ever do is a slim version of such love; but the fragile attempt sometimes makes all the difference.

Here is a church that commits some of its members to regular visits to isolated, fearful, elderly people in rooming houses. There, a missionary priest whose goal is the communication of a new sort of hope to downtown prostitutes. Here, a congregation that works with the local campus minister to be sure that foreign students have enough money to live somewhere other than a slum. And there, a church that supports a dialogue between young Latin American socialists, exiles from their countries, with the leaders of American businesses who are being accused of exploiting landless laborers in both American continents.

Such urban ministries are witnesses on the frontiers where "walls of hostility" divide the human race into warring pieces. The church means to tell the world that the wars are over between God and humanity. And no place is that message more in jeopardy, more in need, more in order, than the great booming, buzzing, pluralistic hubbub of the modern city.

I have sometimes thought that the place to doubt the Incarnation, the place to say definitely that the eighth chapter of Romans was wrong, is the New York subway. Surely God would not pay 50¢ to ride the New York subway! But my wife Peggy wrote a poem the other month about a true incident on that subway. It suggests that God rides the subway, too:

The Spirit of 34th Street

Doors opened with a silent scream,
    like photographs of anguish;
    the subway paused, shed cargo
    and raged on.

She lurched aboard,
    sagged into a vacant seat,
    frail weight of her gray years
    Hunched with cold.
Numb fingers plucked at rags,
    drawn close against raw misery.
    Knuckles, cracked and swollen white,
    clutched into a plea for warmth.

He, dark and lithe,
    swung down the aisle,
    taut jeans dancing
    rhythmically.

> With Latin grace
> he, sidling past
> her patient form,
> in one smooth gesture
> disappeared through subway doors,
> leaving in her lap,
> like folded dove wings,
> his black leather gloves.[5]

One could do worse than incarnate the descent of the Dove in a pair of gloves. But the church's incarnate urban witness, especially in the American south, must be more sophisticated: we must get at the world of social systems. And for that we must face a third question, compounded of current fact and moral vision.

C. *The southern city is rising like a Phoenix from the ashes of an impoverished southern past, at a time when many peoples in the world are seeing the American Phoenix as a hindrance to their own rising. What is the word to the southern city from the Lord who "has put down the mighty from their thrones and exalted those of low degree"?*

The urban south is rising again under the shadow of a great irony. Not long ago Lewis Wilkins addressed a distinguished ecumenical audience on behalf of Southern Presbyterians. Of all the regions of the United States, he said, the south knows best what it is like to be a "Third World Country." In 1933, when Berle and Means published their famous book, *The Modern Corporation and Private Property,*

the 200 largest corporations owned nearly one-fourth of the wealth of America, with 90% located in the North, 4.5% in the South, 5.5% in the West. In 1933, 82% of the savings account dollars in the United States were in the North, 6% were in the South, and 9% in the West. At the same time, the South and West together were producing 95% and 64% of the dollar value of 64 leading agricultural crops in the country.

Does not the statistic ring in one's ears with the tonality of other statistics that are thrown at us these days from

abroad? We are told that the U.S.A. is "a country with 6%
of the world's people consuming 40% of the world's resources." Inequity, disproportion, exploitation . . . words
of international currency these days. But southerners have
had that experience *nationally*. Unique among the regions
of the nation, we have known what military defeat is like,
and in that we have had the most to share with the whole
country on the meaning of its recent defeat in Vietnam.

What will southern Christians make out of this, their
misery-laden entry into the modern industrial world? Well,
said Wilkins perceptively, in 1969

the Southern Presbyterian General Assembly became the first
major American denomination to see the world hunger crisis
rising on the horizon, when it declared this universal human
reality to be a top priority concern of the denomination, for at
least five years and since extended indefinitely. Does this action
contain a visceral sensitivity, born of our own experience as
a church and as a region, to our deep solidarity with the dis-
possessed of the world, a faint memory of what it was like to
stand in those shoes? [6]

Wilkins' question inclines me chiefly toward intercessory
prayer for the southern Christian churches:

—that their ministers and Sunday school teachers will refuse
to imitate the rhetoric of scorn for "welfare chiselers" who
came up from the farm to the city to suffer the starvation of
those who quit school too soon.

—that the comforts of suburban living will not seduce southern
Christians into thinking of suburbs as substitute farmland, when
in fact they are political members of one urban body whose
parts are supposed to have "the same care for each other"
(1 Cor. 12:25).

—that the marvels of profit on investment will not seduce any
of us into uncritical worship of the capitalist or any other system, nor into meek acceptance of taxation policies that fatten
suburban schools at the price of starving inner city schools, or
political policies that fuel defense spending at the price of

threatening every city of the nation with a version of the devastated landscape of the South Bronx.

That sort of intercessory prayer is one with the confessions and petitions many of us should raise for ourselves to the Lord of cities and every other human construct:

Lord, for the profit of your kingdom, we are often unprofitable servants; give us a new vision of what the abundant life is really about.

FROM SOCIAL VISION TO SOCIAL CHANGE: THREE URBAN MINISTRIES

What might it really be about in urban terms? What would be some ministries of promised redemption in the midst of our new urban, secular urban setting? Some things that move beyond judgment, beyond even the hailing of the city of God from afar? I will dare to be painfully specific. It will give you much to argue about. Practical proposals always betray that two-edged sword at work in a theory. Said Kurt Lewin, "Nothing is so practical as a good theory." Having always regarded the justice, the mercy, and the power of God in Jesus Christ as a "good theory," I recommend to you these possible social-political-ethical embodiments of that theory in the ministry of our urban churches.

THE HOUSING AGONY

It is time for southern churches to address locally, regionally, and nationally the scandal of deteriorating housing in our cities. Food, a place to sleep, and someone to love are not a bad first list of what it takes to keep human life human. But the places to sleep in this country, in our cities especially, are getting older, more expensive, and harder to find. Here we are the richest country in the world, and only 25 percent of our population can now afford to

buy the alleged American dream of a private home. Here
we are, spending billions on questionable protection for
our cities from the devastation of nuclear warfare, while
we build southern cities on the same principle that the older
northern cities were built: Let the rich move on to better
housing further away from the city core, let the poor move
in behind them, until the original housing investment has
been many times recouped, and the most profit lies in
writing off the remaining hulks as a tax loss or as an object
of "arrangeable" arson.

A complex urban problem. Do we doubt that it is too
complex a problem for the Lord of cities? Or so intransi-
gent that the massed intelligence, know-how, and compassion of the financially astute and politically powerful
can do nothing about it? Incredible! Credible, rather, is
the suggestion of a certain Presbyterian elder in Atlanta
some years ago that church people literally break new
ground for housing by offering some of their ample suburban church properties to the city government for the
building of subsidized housing for people of low and modest
income. The suggestion, at last check, had not gotten very
far in Atlanta. After all, it cuts across the assumption of
class-segregation that structures the real estate market of
the southern and every other city in the United States.

At one time southerners were rather proud that the rich
and the poor, even the slave and the free, lived within shouting distance of each other. Now we are too far apart in
our cities even to shout. My good friend Will Kennedy
relates his premature delight, as a new member of the U.S.
Navy, in striking up a friendly conversation with a young
black man from Spartanburg, S.C. It was home town for
both of them. But to their mutual chagrin, as they talked,
they could identify not a single person whom both of them
knew. The most obvious reason was the structure of housing and class segregation in the cities of the south.

Can you read what the New Testament says about the
church, or the city of God, and be comfortable with all

this? Must we let money, race, and class wall us off from our neighbors? Men and women were never meant to bow down before three idols—so says the Bible from *Genesis* to *Revelation.*

THE WELFARE OF THE POOR

It is time as well for Christians to conceive justice and mercy in the concrete terms of a reform in the so-called welfare system of this country. Among the cherished convictions that southern history makes it hard for many of us to revise is the individualism that has inclined many southern factory workers, for example, against the labor union. We also show our regional individualism in our tendency to resist seeing our social problems in the south as part of national and international problems. The time has come for Calvinist universalism to triumph over regionalism on such points.

Living in New York City as I do, the problem of jobless poor people readily looms in my imagination as a national and international problem. For a long time, the south has exported poor people to the cities of the north, especially New York City, where the welfare laws and budgets make living in Harlem more attractive than living in the Delta. It is fashionable for many of us to forget to award to New York a badge of moral honor on this point.

Who has a right to boast about the low levels of state welfare budgets in the southeastern U.S.? Granting that the rich northern cities have profited unjustly for a century from their commercial relations with the south, shall we condemn them for spending part of that profit on the cause of making life in cities more tolerable for our exported poor?

Such questions are rhetorical for the Christian conscience: blame the New Yorkers for their political corruption, but not for their political compassion for the poor! The questions call for something more than a rhetorical answer, however: they call for new assessments of the structured moral faults in the American economy, and for brave facing of a question never before faced much by Americans southern or northern: How shall we distribute among one another the limited resources of this and other continents?

The oil in Texas, the land around Atlanta, the oranges in Florida: who will be included, who excluded from some part of that wealth? Such questions come partly out of the current international collision between socialism and capitalism; but they should come more profoundly out of a Christian reading of the Bible and its "bias toward the weak." Not long ago Robert Bellah in his book, *The Broken Covenant,* looked back at the Calvinist Puritans who came to both New England and Virginia, and at the balance between the individual and the community in American social philosophies. We live, he says, in a time calling for new religious-cultural vision.

If we are to transcend the limitations of American culture and society it can only be on the basis of an imaginative vision that can generate an experience of inner conversion and lead to a new form of (social) covenant. . . . The period of the late 20th-century America will not be overcome by everyone doing his or her "own thing," but through the discovery of cultural and social forms that can give the disciplined basis for a new degree of moral freedom.[7]

Robert Bellah was raised a Presbyterian. His language here resonates with the polarities of Calvinism: conversion . . . covenant . . . discipline . . . freedom. Toward the end of his book he puts our national need into a prescription: We must begin to disregard some taboos of the past and "begin talking about and helping to delineate a distinctively American socialism." [7]

Do southern Christians have a contribution to make to such delineation? I am not sure. But among those who might, are the people who lead city churches, for they are likely to be observant enough to see that no mere tinkering with a welfare bureaucracy will solve the larger problems of inflation, resource scarcity, and the decreasing need of mechanized industry for masses of wage workers. These are big problems of justice, politics, and technical wisdom. Such problems require people who are unafraid of new horizons.

Christians have always specialized in being just such people. Those Calvinists called Southern Presbyterians and Southern Baptists are heirs of a tradition that dares to propose new patterns for entire societies. Calvin did not shrink from prescribing reforms for the whole city of Geneva, and he was the most international of sixteenth century reformers. What looked like pretentious defiance of tradition in him was in fact subservience to the two-edged Word of God, who humbles the proud protectors of privileged systems and lifts up the poor and the meek who are supposed to inherit the earth.

The modern American urban church has little access to the levers of power available to Calvin, "that Frenchman" in Geneva. In religion-suspicious secular America we are shoved somewhat to the edges of urban society. Our powers seem minimal. But the edges of society have always been a good place for prophets to be. Out there, they can scan the whole of things and see futures beyond the busy preoccupations of specialists in their secure niches. *Why not an urban church that specializes in liberating its members to dream new dreams, see new visions, and nourish new concrete systems for making the human city a place which welcomes, rather than scorns, its poorest citizens?*

A NEW GLOBAL COMMUNITY

In that connection, it is time for at least one more ministry among southern urban Christians: *The local urban church must rise to the promise of the secular ecumenism in the modern city; the church must pioneer in the making*

*of humane intersections between the local and the global
human community.* You can travel to many a foreign country these days by simply staying home in a mid-sized city
and talking with its stream of visitors from around the
world. Leaders of multinational corporations claim that
they are the most truly international systems in the world
today; that they are in the process of outmoding the na-
tion-state. Indeed, in cities where those corporations are
located (one thinks of New York, Atlanta, and Houston),
one can breathe the culture of another continent by simply walking down the hall or going to a certain lecture
across town at the university.

What is the church going to make of all this in a concrete urban ministry? I can think of three parabolic il-
lustrations:

(1) Atlanta Presbytery invites a young woman from
Ghana to come as counter-missionary to Georgia, and she
is immediately a link between Presbyterians and the large
group of African students who study in that city. (2) Four
Puerto Rican seminary students spend a year at Union
Seminary in New York, partly to forge some links between our school and that portion of the international
Spanish community which lives a block away from our
institutional front door. (3) Yet more ambitiously and
courageously, Mecklenburg Presbytery, Myers Park Presbyterian Church, and the Covenant Presbyterian Church of
Charlotte organize a million-dollar community development program in Haiti, with the help of a Church World
Service expert from the Middle East, a Haitian sociologist,
and many committed villagers in Haiti who would rather
live well fed in Haiti than migrate hungry to New York or
Charlotte.[8]

Such projects spring from a vision of world-wide human need in the context of urban church capacity to make
partial response to that need. Whatever flaws such projects
may have, they are congenial signs left behind on the
roads that Christians ought to be traveling these days along

their pilgrim way. "Here we have no lasting city, but we seek the city which is to come" (Heb. 13:14). Happy is that human city salted and enlightened by such a heavenly vision that its citizens are always on their way toward something better. It is the work of urban Christians to be sure that their urban neighbors have a chance to glimpse, and to be obedient to, such a vision.

NOTES

1. Willie Morris, *North Toward Home*. Boston: Houghton Mifflin Co., 1967. Pp. 370–71.

2. John Egerton, "Looks Like the Mason-Dixon Line Was Erased," *New York Times,* May 24, 1977.

3. See Sam Bass Warner, *The Urban Wilderness*. New York: Harper and Row, 1972.

4. *North Toward Home,* p. 347.

5. Published in *The Christian Century,* August, 1977.

6. Lewis Wilkins, "The Present Profile of Ecumenical Relations in the Presbyterian Church U.S.," in *Mid-Stream: An Ecumenical Journal,* Vol. XV, #1, (January 1976), pp. 38–39, 44–45.

7. Robert N. Bellah, *The Broken Covenant*. New York: The Seabury Press, 1975. Pp. 85–86, 137.

8. For a longer description of the Charlotte project, and a more systematic account of the theology and strategy that informs the perspectives of this entire presentation, see the book, *Is There Hope for the City?* by Donald W. Shriver, Jr. and Karl A. Ostrom, (Philadelphia: The Westminster Press, 1977).

The Flavor of
New Directions

*Howard C. Blake **

10.

Styles in Christian Missions

ALL THE PEOPLE OF GOD IS THE BASIC meaning of the laity. All the People of God working in the world creatively and effectively is the deceptively simple concept which is here advocated.

Most thoughtful church leaders are increasingly convinced that we have a God-given responsibility for the world around us. Only a few of the more pietistic types would still proclaim a withdrawal into the church, seen as an ark, a fortress, or a colony of heaven. The vital question is not so much what should be done in the world. It is clear that a wide variety of mission programs and service projects is the order of day. Moreover, we specifically encourage all the worthwhile and faithful work which has been and is continuing to be performed in the name of Christ and his church.

* Howard C. Blake spent many years in Europe in Christian service before he became Pastor and Executive Presbyter in South Texas Presbytery. Howard is well-beloved by many on both sides of the Atlantic. His brother is Eugene Carson Blake, former stated clerk of the United Presbyterian church. Peggy Blake is an outstanding Christian worker. In active retirement, they live in Placitos, New Mexico.

The crucial question which we are trying to address is, "How can Christian service in the world be more effective?"

For example, a few years ago while I was a pastor, one of the elders, who was on the local school board, asked me whether he should attend the school board meeting or attend the church session meeting. After a thoughtful conversation, we mutually agreed that his task was to be a conscientious school board member. Expanding that rather simple idea, I have become increasingly more convinced that if the message and virtues of the gospel are to have an impact on the world, it would be by the faithful laity who are already working in all the corporate structures of the world.

The church needs its dedicated laity to work in the church. But the new direction and new style of Christian mission is the challenge to be an active, concerned Christian in the world. What does it mean to be a Christian school board member, or a Christian business person, or a Christian farmer?

The new concept began to grow. First, it became clear that the sincere but rather ineffective methods of the past were to be avoided. Helping people is a notoriously difficult task, but there needs to be a consistent life behind the motivation to service. To force help upon people is hardly the way. "Lady Bountiful" distributing Christmas baskets in her limousine is not really helping the poor, is it? There is the case of a missionary giving the natives portions of scripture in a language they can't read. Trying to be of service on our terms and the arrogance of "we know best what you need" is largely discredited.

Secondly, a whole new approach is emerging which is focused on helping people on their terms, not ours, and in enlisting their participation. More recently there have been even more subtle understandings of the need to preserve dignity and self-determination in those whom we would help. No longer does a trained mission worker move into the ghetto and announce that there he will establish a child day care center, simply because he knows one is needed. A new humility is becoming a part of the "how" as we inquire first what the people feel is their real need. Then we insist on their right to share fully in the leadership and responsibility for whatever projects are to be undertaken.

THE STRUCTURES

The shift from the personal to the corporate is a giant step in the right direction. Personal evangelism and commitment to Jesus Christ as Lord and Savior are necessary qualities of the effective Christian. We strongly affirm the absolute necessity for personal direction and personal motivation. However, personal morality and personal dedication are not enough. When we begin to take seriously the implications of the gospel for the way we live in the modern world, it becomes clear that there has always been interaction between church and world. In the first three centuries of the Christian era the spread of the gospel profoundly affected the way the world was organized and ruled. After Constantine, the official adoption of Christianity as a state religion deeply affected the church. There have always been and there continues to be mutual influences in both directions. The historians are still arguing about the details of this mutual influence between the church and culture, and will likely continue to explore this fascinating relationship.

In our own times we are witnessing a new phase in these interrelationships. This new phase has been chiefly focused on the what and why. However, the thrust of the new laity is to call attention to the "how" in more creative and effective ways.

THE ADVERSARY STANCE

Most Christian leaders have come to realize that merely treating the symptoms of the social diseases of poverty, hunger, injustice, pollution, prejudice, and racism is not enough. Somehow the root causes of the various most difficult problems require our concerned attention. While almost everyone will agree with this assessment, certainly it is seen as not new or startlingly original. Again the question of "how" is central.

The all too familiar kinds of protest, both violent and nonviolent, are freshly etched on our minds and hearts. As a result of these many types of protest, the churchmen involved have inevitably come to assume an adversary stance of confrontation toward those in positions of authority and responsibility. The value of such protests is for others to determine. One difficulty with such a stance is that probably the vast majority of the top leaders consider themselves also as good Christians. There is nothing new in sincere Christians disagreeing with each other. But deliberately to alienate the leadership of industry and government is in my judgment a serious error of style and tactics.

IS THERE A BETTER WAY?

The answer is yes, I think there is. While certain types of protest may have been advisable in some particular cases, I have been reaching for another method of approach in the practical application of the ethical issues involved. It is probable that those outside the establishment have made a valuable contribution by seeing the issues with keener discernment. However, in my opinion the time has come to project a new image of support and encouragement to those in leadership positions. Perhaps those in authority have not taken the time and considerable effort required to reflect on the social moral issues. In that case we, as church leaders, can also blame ourselves for not having done enough to help in clarifying these serious issues.

Perhaps too much of our time and attention has been taken up with keeping the wheels of the institutional church spinning smoothly. The Lord knows we need all the help we can get in organizing the church activities properly. The able laity might get the impression that our only interest in them is to enlist a bit of their spare time and some of their spare money to help us in running the church. Too often we seem content if the laity is willing to give us only bits and pieces of their lives.

The net result of all this is that we fail to realize that these men and women out there in the world *are* the church. It seems so easy to let the situation become a matter of *them* and *us*. The adversary posture thus ill becomes us. *They* are not the problem, it is *us*. While it is easier and certainly safer to be content with running the church, it is less than faithful not to be involved in the world. The people of God are already in the world and deserve the prayers, comfort, and best attention of the whole church.

The reasons that we are being led to this position of support and encouragement are many. One of the most common is to decide that effective change for the better is basically impossible on any voluntary basis. For example, a study document of the French Protestant Federation, *The Church and the Powers,* puts this case very strongly. "In short, it is vain to expect any reform of the system. Its defects, far from being temporary aberrations are inherent in neocapitalism, so much so as often to constitute its very foundation." Not everyone comes out so bluntly as these logical French Protestants, but there are a good many people who are convinced that change, while desirable, is virtually impossible.

Such a cultural pessimism is hardly appropriate for the people of God who confess trust in the God who loves the world enough to send his Son to save it. Even if there is much evidence of evil running rampant in the world, a strong faith in the sovereign Lord of us all must seek other alternatives. To cave in with despair and withdraw, or to foster violent revolution do not exhaust the possibilities. There is another way.

A NEW WIND

There is a new wind blowing now in the church. This
refreshing breath of the Holy Spirit is repairing old foundations, restoring new vitality, healing old wounds, and renewing fresh commitment. The new evangelicals in large
number are becoming more involved in the application of
the gospel, as well as in the *experience* of it. The new
liberals are beginning to see the necessity for a solid theological and Bible base for their vigorous social actions. The
gospel is alive and well when it is heard both for the inner
self and for the desperate plight of the world. Producing
social change is inseparably linked with finding new reser-
voirs of spiritual power.

The so-called "two party system" in all the churches is
increasingly being viewed as a false division. To love God
means to love our neighbors. To love our neighbors points
to the necessity of loving God.

In both cases the newer trend toward rapprochement
represents more of a return to Biblical principles than to
a departure from those principles. For example, the evangelical tradition in its early days was at the forefront of
social reforms. The struggles against the British slave trade,
child labor, American slavery, and war as an instrument of
national interest were led by fervent evangelicals. Dwight
L. Moody and Henry Drummond both were powerful evangelical leaders.

In his essay entitled *The City Without a Church,* Drummond speaks forcibly, "If anyone wishes to know what he
can do to help on the work of God in the world let him
make a City, or a street, or a house of a City. Men com-
plain of the indefiniteness of religion. There are thousands
ready in their humble measure to offer some personal
service for the good of men, but they do not know where to
begin. Let me tell you where to begin, where Christ told
His disciples to begin, at the nearest City. I promise you
that before one week's work is over you will never again be

haunted by the problem of the indefiniteness of Christianity. You will see so much to do, so many actual things to be set right, so many merely material conditions to alter, so much striving with employers of labour, and City councils, and trade agitators, and Boards, and Vestries, and Committees; so much pure unrelieved uninspiring hard work, that you will begin to wonder whether in all this naked realism you are on holy ground at all. Do not be afraid of missing Heaven in seeking a better earth. The distinction between secular and sacred is a confusion and not a contrast; and it is only because the secular is so intensely sacred that so many eyes are blind before it. The really secular thing in life is the spirit which despises under that name what is but part of the everywhere present work and will of God. Be sure that, down to the last and pettiest detail, all that concerns a better world is the direct concern of Christ." [1]

On the other hand, Walter Rauschenbusch (1861–1918) is generally regarded as the founder and leading exponent of the social gospel. One of his major interests was to hold together the spiritual roots and the social passion of the gospel. In his *Christianizing the Social Order,* he wrote, "It is not this thing or that thing our nation needs, but a new mind and heart, a new conception of the way we all ought to live together, a new conviction about the worth of a human life and the use God wants us to make of our own lives. We want a revolution both inside and outside. We want a moral renovation of public opinion and a revival of religion. A righteous public opinion may bring the proudest sinner low. But the most pervasive scrutiny, a control which follows our actions to their fountain head where the desires and motives of the soul are born, is exerted only by personal religion." [2]

In an article on Rauschenbusch, Robert T. Handy writes, "After Rauschenbusch's death the social gospel and the liberal theology on which it was based developed in several different and not wholly consistent directions, none of which would probably have had his full approval. The basic synthesis for which he labored did not prove to be lasting. Some representatives of the social gospel tended toward a humanistic orientation and in their attention to the social minimized the religious; others focused their attention on one or two major social problems and neglected the larger scene." [3]

A NEW APPROACH

The reaching for a new balance between the personal and the social is illustrated by the so-called "Chicago Declaration," written by a group called "Evangelicals for Social Action." It reads in part, "We acknowledge that we have failed to condemn the exploitation of racism at home and abroad by our economic system. Before God and a billion hungry neighbors, we must rethink our values regarding our present standard of living and promote more just acquisition and distribution of the world's resources." It goes on to list nine main areas of social concern.

On the other hand, Richard Neuhaus and William Sloane Coffin, Jr., two of the most fiery advocates of social causes in recent history, were among a group which put out the so-called "Hartford Statement." Francine du Plessix Gray interviewed Neuhaus about this and wrote in *The New York Times,* "Hartford's message, in his view, was that social action would be more effective and lasting if grounded in deeper spiritual conviction. Above all it was a critique of what he called 'the cultural captivity of religion.' He cited the enormous disaffection of parishioners from those liberal churches that emphasize extensive social programs at the expense of piety. 'After all, what do most people see as the function of religion?' he asked. 'They see prayer, worship, transcendence, eternal life, and they're right,' he added triumphantly." [4]

The so-called conservatives are calling for more social

action. The so-called social activists are calling for more attention to the transcendence of God. I think this is healthy and most encouraging. We need both the spiritual and the social elements of the gospel.

A FRESH ATTACK

After several years of discussion all over Europe and much prayer and thoughtful consideration, an invitation was issued to leaders from the evangelical family of churches, from the traditional Protestant cluster of churches, and from the Roman Catholic Church. The concepts of mutual cooperation among all the Christians, and the balanced approach between church and world were the basic motivations of the conference held at the University of Dallas in June, 1976. Seldom had the evangelicals and the traditional Protestants been drawn together. Almost never had all three been related, even in such an informal way.

Since Vatican Council II the laity movement in the Catholic Church has been gaining vigor and strength. The leaders of the Laity Council, an official organ of the Roman Curia, cabled greetings. Officers of the National Council of Catholic Laity were present and played a major role of leadership.

Best of all, the three types of participants showed a new willingness to listen to each other. On the basis of this kind of united effort, something quite new and exciting may emerge in the church's laity as a whole. Many kinds of follow-through are now being planned and the practical results are being realized. This book is one of them.

The other significant feature is that the conference was international, for several leaders from Europe were present, including Mark Gibbs from England and Hans Ruede Weber from Switzerland. Both were speakers at the conference.

A NEW STYLE

The question now is: will it be possible for life-changing to take place on a far deeper level than has often been the case? When a person makes a decision to let God take charge, it needs to be far more than a verbal acquiescence, far more than the giving up of crippling habits, far more than the rebuilding of family relationships. When we aim at changing structures through the action of those who lead them, it will mean first of all an understanding of the real situation and of all the costly issues involved. It will mean in the end a willingness to risk everything, job and career, position and power, if a new God-given force is to be pitted against the pressures of a well-organized oligarchy. Readiness to sacrifice the excesses of our out of balance standards of comfort and wealth in favor of a fair deal to workers, the public, other nations, all may be necessary. This is just the sort of conversion that many have deemed impossible.

Certainly no serious effort has been made to work in this way up to now with any feeling that it might be a viable way to go. It will be a daring and new way. It will require new qualities in us of the church, a radically new style.

One of the elements will be a new humility. It will never happen as long as we come as adversaries, arrogant in the certainty that we know what is best. Suppose we draw the lesson from our experience in the ghetto and use the same humble approach we have learned there. We then can listen to these men and women who carry responsibility. We can show a willingness to help them to fulfill their God-given vocations more satisfactorily than at present. For we shall find that few men or women are really satisfied with the present situation. Of course, if we attack them, they close the gate and admit only what they are forced to admit. If we allow ourselves to be vulnerable, we can learn how these gates can be unlocked. A new factor can be introduced.

We can be supportive rather than combative, encouraging rather than accusing, gracious rather than demanding, humble rather than authoritative. This kind of change is never going to be accomplished by psychological manipulation. It will not come as a result of group dynamics. Nor can it be induced by a winning personality. Reasoning and argument do not have that power. Change of the level we are talking about will only come through the Holy Spirit. It may not be dramatic in the way it happens, but it will still be a miracle.

LAY ACADEMIES

Look for a bit at how other church bodies are already working. In Europe there are scores of lay academies operated by or in close conjunction with the churches. Many different people have attempted to transplant these institutions to American soil, but so far the lay academy movement has never taken root over here. The one most outstanding impression from scores of visits to the academies is the enormous scope of their concerns. Conferences are held week after week, in place after place, on matters that lie at the heart of concerns for the world's functioning. Not only are the topics chosen the right ones, but the men and women invited to participate are those already deeply involved, exactly the ones who can best benefit from an exchange of ideas and experiences in their own fields.

ACTION GROUPS

The Catholics generally work through movements rather than institutions, and there is a formidable list of such lay movements, the Christian Life communities of the Jesuits, the Movements for a Better World of Father Lombardi, the Grail (a women's movement), the Cursillos, to mention only a few. Once I called on the head of the Christian Life Movement in Great Britain, Father Ralph

Eastwell, S. J. He welcomed me in his small office away up in the north end of London, not far from Golder's Green.

Father Eastwell told of the growth of these small groups, which had been simply prayer groups 200 years ago, when they were known as "sodalities." Now they meet regularly to discuss and to listen and to pray about the Christian in relation to the world. Conferences are concerned with the Common Market, the welfare state, liberation and development, and many other matters where Christian thinking is needed. The aim of these groups is not so much to lead people to specific action as to form individual character so that Christians will act on their convictions rather than from lesser motives. Groups, some interparish, others not, are limited to ten persons. Six to ten is the average size. There are some 1700 of them in Great Britain. They meet weekly and divide their time, half of it devoted to spiritual preparation and formation, and half to application and action. From time to time larger conferences and retreats are held. Each group member is supposed to make at least one retreat a year.

Another kind of small study/action/fellowship group style of work was headed by Pat Keegan, a layman, also in London. He had a most unimposing office on the third floor of a small row house far out Clapham Road in South London. He creates and supplies materials for small groups of lay people. Nearly 2,000 small groups draw inspiration, instruction, plans of action, and vigorous spiritual life out of this unlikely headquarters. An almost unique feature of this set of groups, called "Family and Social Action," is that the sponsoring organization is practically anonymous. The average member of a parish group will probably know that there are eight or ten such groups meeting regularly in his parish. He will not know that there are hundreds and hundreds of other groups like his in other parishes. In this respect Pat Keegan's work is more of a church program than an independent movement. Pat works through the bishops and local priests, supplies the ideas and tools and lets the priests take the credit. Not surprisingly, he gets much more enthusiastic cooperation from the parish priests than do other movements which are clearly labeled as outside the diocesan structure.

CHARACTERISTICS WE NEED

It is time now to recapitulate and to draw together a list of the elements needed for an effective style. Some have been mentioned already. Some will be new. It is not always easy to separate the "what" from the "how," but I will try to stick to qualities. If some of the "what" creeps in, I hope the reader will forgive!

(1) There is that element of *consistency* in the life behind whatever we do.

(2) *Identification* of ourselves with those whom we wish to help will be vital. No Lady Bountifuls, please!

(3) *Clarity* in our understanding of the difference between gospel principle and cultural trappings. This will mean that we recognize that God does not belong to the Republican Party. Nor is he a Socialist, either!

(4) *Humility* will be central and one of the most difficult qualities to live. C. S. Lewis properly identified the pride of knowing best, or "playing God," as the central sin.

(5) A *positive attitude* toward people will be a good starting place. This can never mean simply ruling out confrontation. At times that is the most loving and positive tactic there is. But it seldom helps to begin that way.

(6) *Faith* that the God who made us and redeemed us is also powerful to help us change structures as well is essential.

(7) *Wholeness* is our gospel, being fully aware of both the vertical and horizontal aspects of its content, will help us unite the church and the people in it.

(8) The *willingness to listen* is one of those rare qualities that marks a catalyst, a person who knows something of the art of changing lives and of changing systems, too.

(9) Those qualities of being *supportive, encouraging, gracious* will have a place.

(10) *Dependence* on the miracle-working power of the Holy Spirit, rather than on techniques we think we have mastered, is again one of the most important qualities we can find.

(11) Insistence on *quality* in all our thinking and working is highly important. Shoddy or cheap schemes will never do it. No shooting from the hip.

(12) Aim at *decision* and *action* without ever being content with cerebration and mere words, which at times can be sterile.

(13) *Freedom* from the tyranny of bricks and mortar will be vital. We cannot have *real estate* dictating policy. (This often happens when the fact of owning a conference center demands constant use of the buildings.) There are plenty of places available when we need to meet.

(14) A *deliberately positive attitude* toward other individuals and groups working in the name of Christ never seems to come easily. It is often especially difficult to appreciate the virtues of those whose aim and style most nearly resemble our own.

(15) *Flexibility* in the tactics we use is vital. No one patent scheme fits all situations, and no one way of working will meet the variety of needs.

(16) Interest always in *persons before things* will be a guideline.

(17) *Willingness to be unseen,* letting credit go where it may, will be difficult but urgently needed. It may often mean working through existing groups and other agencies, rather than some action that bears our trademark.

(18) *Sensitivity* to the guidance of the Holy Spirit will mean more than all the human wisdom we can muster.

(19) We will need to remember that problem-solving only prepares the way for cooperating with God's *creative activity* in finding the new thing he wants done in the world.

(20) We will need to be free to choose the point of attack, taking the initiative ourselves. We cannot just sit back and hope that the people most in need of help will ask for it. Nor can we help only those who have the funds and want to hire us. Many good works miss the goal because they deal only with those who pay the registration fee.

(21) *Lay leadership* is a rare thing in Christian activity. An overwhelming number of institutions for the laity or lay movements are headed by clerics. Let's avoid that trap and insist on having lay men and women in the leadership.

NOTES

1. Henry Drummond, *The Greatest Thing in the World.* Glasgow: Collins, 1964. P. 86.
2. Walter Rauschenbusch, *Christianizing the Social Order.* New York: Macmillan, 1912. P. 459.
3. Martin E. Marty and Dean G. Peerman, *A Handbook of Christian Theologians.* Cleveland and New York: World, 1965. P. 209.
4. *The New York Times,* 27 June 1976. "To March or Not to March," Francis du Plessix Gray.

A. Fred Swearingen *

11.

Worship and Service

I BELIEVE THAT HOW A PERSON WORSHIPS is vitally connected with how a person lives. The worship of the faithful is basically an experience of the whole person in rediscovering who the person is. The quest for identity and for a new appreciation of the profound depth of human nature is one major goal of corporate worship. The quest for a life-inspiring vision of who God is, is one other major goal in worship. A fresh awareness of self-identity and a transforming relationship with Almighty God are thus linked inseparably together like Siamese twins. To try to separate the two is to kill both.

The purpose of this essay is to reach for a more vital connection between worship and service. Worship is asking the question, "Who am I?" Service is asking the question, "What am I to do?" As those who want to be faithful, we do not ask one and then the other question, but rather we ask both questions at the same time. We gain insight into who we are as a servant people of God as we perform loving and supportive deeds. We understand more clearly

* A. FRED SWEARINGEN is pastor of Parkway Presbyterian Church, Corpus Christi, Texas. A graduate of Yale Divinity School, he taught worship and liturgy at Austin Seminary, Austin, Texas.

what and how we can best serve by rediscovering in worship who we are.

THE SIGNIFICANCE OF THE "LITURGICAL MOVEMENT"

The word, liturgy, literally means the "work of the people." As a pastor, one of my primary services is that of liturgist. As one who leads the people in worship, it is important to me to keep being reminded that I am one of the people of God who participates in worship. So I am personally involved, as is anyone who is worshiping on either side of the sacred altar. *Please* take your own worship personally.

The primary aim of the liturgical movement in the last few years has been to affect a "coming alive" in new and fresh expressions of corporate worship. All communities of faith, Christian and Jewish, have undergone sharp changes in the *forms* of service and in the *manner* in which those services are conducted.

The movement toward revision has cleared away much of the stiff formalism and perfunctory performances on the part of the clergy who too often have celebrated as if the congregation did not exist. A more human and humanizing style of worship has been emerging. The crucial shift from mere formality, even in those traditions who have been rigidly formal in their informality, to a disciplined spontaneity on the part of the pastor and on the part of the people is one positive sign of solid encouragement. A new theological perspective which accents the joy of the Easter triumph, tempered by the severe suffering of Good Friday, has largely displaced a guilt-ridden, propitiatory sacrifice heavy with funereal tones. With lay participation increasing, what used to be a spectacle performed solely by the pastor has been replaced by opportunities for the people to express their own relationship with God and with each other. One of the strongest elements of the liturgical revolution has been the fresh opportunity for the spiritual and

theological renewal of the laity, thus making corporate
worship "the people's service."

SEEING BEYOND THE STAINED GLASS WINDOWS

It is quite significant that the worship of the church
has been called the worship service. Such wording is provi-
dential because it points beyond itself. People are not seen
exclusively as isolated individuals, but are being seen as
authentic persons, who share a mutual responsibility for
society. God is not perceived so much as One who is dis-
tant, out there, or in heaven, but rather God is increasingly
being perceived as One who is near, here, and right now.
While careful to appreciate the transcendence of God, the
new concept of real worship feels the immanence of God
as a trusted friend and faithful companion. Isn't this what
the incarnation means? "The word became flesh and dwelt
among us . . ." (John 1:14).

Modern English with its contemporary style of expression has moved us beyond the mock-gothic toward a living
language of reality. This, in turn, has encouraged a style
which understands worship to be a call to engage the
present world, not to withdraw from it.

A new vision of what John 3:16,17 means is a case in
point. Following perhaps the best-known and most-loved
verse in the entire New Testament, we read, "For God
sent the Son into the world, not to condemn the world,
but that the world might be saved through him."

If God is present in the world, surely the faithful are
called to serve in the world. Where else can we serve?

FROM WORSHIP TO ETHICS

The first business of the Christian faith is to help the
people of God capture a vision of how life can be with God
in Christ. Then on the upbeat the task of faith is to help
the people make ethical choices and to perform moral

deeds. I am not suggesting that churches have not been moral enough, nor do I believe that we should "interfere" more in people's lives. Moral advice is free enough, and worth about what it costs. I am amazed at the arrogance of the church sometimes when she pontificates on almost every subject. The laity are already in the world and need help in clarifying the issues, not in ponderous pronouncements, especially in "holier than thou" put-downs.

When are we going to learn that to petrify Christian ethics into little routines and the endless mimeographing of rules is to sterilize it, thus assuring its ineffectiveness? No! The first thing to show our children and our world is the vision of God and the adventure of living by faith. If we can share the quality of life we have, then we can see beyond the stained glass myopia to a faithful people who are free to trust the faithfulness of God, rather than their own. You see! To be moral means to trust God as we experience him in worship and as we serve him in the world with dignity and with responsibility.

THE WORD/DEED TENSION

In worship it is possible to see the unity between the word and the deed. Christ is the Word and that Word is the deed. The drama of Good Friday and Easter is played out on the stage of real life as deed. Christ did something because he was something, unique and ultimately redemptive.

Somehow we have misunderstood this vital unity and have set up a false division. Perhaps the strength and the appeal of the charismatic type of worship is a good example of "doing" something in worship. Freedom to express the feelings and the emotions is one important element in worship. We know that every faith which has made its way into history was born in ecstasy and seeks to nurture it. But emotional ecstasy is not all there is in worship. There is also content of commitment, generated from a living presence and the deeply human response to the deeds and to the word of Emmanuel, God with us.

So on the one hand the charismatics stress the emotional involvement so much that they tend not to remember the quiet assurance. "Be still and know that I am God. . . ." On the other hand the traditionalists seem to worship the past more than the alive present. So at this deeper level the word/deed tension needs to be preserved because the church desperately needs both the solid content and the emotionally involved whole person. One tends to feed on the other so that they are mutually interdependent. So the word/deed tension is not so much on the surface of experience as opposed to action, but rather a deep dimension is revealed when the people of God are free enough to do in worship as well as to "taste and see that the Lord is good."

THE BEST IS YET TO BE

Robert Browning has said something to us in this classic sentence. My criticism of the traditionalist who seeks to preserve the values of the past is mild because we need to remember with grateful hearts what God has done. My supportive criticism of the charismatics is filled with love because their emphasis on the present is valid and necessary. Both are partially on target. However, I do not think the core of true faith is in either the past or in the present. The core of true faith points to the future. Our Lord is futuristic and speaks of what is ahead. A creative blend of the past and the present yields a triumphant hope of the future.

This is expressly not an apocalyptic form of idealism. Rather, it is attempting to be a clarion call to hope in the promises of the living Lord who is constantly urging the people of God onward and upward.

GRASSHOPPERS FOR HIS PEOPLE OF FAITH

I have been fascinated over the years with the Exodus event. Perhaps the journey out of Egypt and through the desert is an apt illustration of the profound depth of the true worship experience.

The report came back that the land of promise was filled with giants, those with long necks who were fearsome warriors. Fear and despair are the real enemies of faith.

It has been said that the worst thing Adolph Hitler did to the professing Christians, both clergy and laity, was to make them afraid. I remember the "night of the long knives" when thousands of Christians were brutally murdered back in the 1930s in Germany. I also remember the "Holocaust." So fear is not imaginary or unreal. However, the debilitating panic and the paralyzing terror was worse, because the credibility of religious faith was weakened, and it produces what Jim McCord calls the "grasshopper neurosis."

There are many giants in our land today. Giants filled with power and evil. Giants fearsome and dedicated to protecting their self-interest, even at the expense of the whole society, are stalking the land of promise. You know who some of these long-necked giants are. The majority of ten to two brought back to Moses a pessimistic, cautious to say the least, report. "There are giants in the land; we were in our own sight as grasshoppers, and so we were to them."

Nothing is so devastating as self-defeat. "We were in our own sight as grasshoppers" simply haunts my conscience. For example, have we really left Egypt—fleshpots and all? Our bodies like our common ancestors are in the desert *on the way*. But where are our souls, our minds, or our true selves? We cannot stay in Egypt, nor can we stay in the desert. We dare not believe the majority report. Yet we are ambivalent, hesitating, waiting.

Listen to me! All the advance from the slavery of Egypt
to the freedom of the promised land, literally and figura-
tively has been motivated by faith, not by sight. We cannot
live without faith. But we are few in number, comparatively
ill-prepared to weather the fierce storms. Yes, but the God
of Abraham, Isaac, and Jacob is calling all the people of
God to trust him. He provided Moses and his people with
manna. He guided them with cloud by day and fiery pillar
by night. Do you honestly believe he will do less for us?
"As I was with Moses, so I shall be with you," saith the
Lord.

WHAT IS AHEAD FOR US?

If this biased interpretation of a 58-year-old parish pastor, written as bits and pieces of a mosaic, is true at all,
then we need to worship the Holy One with sincere rever-
ence. We need to treasure the ministry of all God's people;
we need to reaffirm the basic meaning of the church as a
worshiping, loving, and serving community of faith. And
we need to reassert the claims of Jesus Christ as Lord over
all creation. Indeed, we need to rediscover the vision of
the suffering servant who calls us out of darkness into his
marvelous light. Dare we do less? Can we do more?

WITHOUT A VISION THE PEOPLE PERISH

(1) God has made each one of us a person of unique
worth, fit to worship.

(2) Our self-worth is strongly affirmed in a loving and
serving church in the presence of Almighty God
and in the presence of a supportive community of
faith.

(3) As we are secure enough to reveal ourselves, we in-
vite others to share the rare gifts of faith, hope, and
love.

(4) The way to call forth the best in each of us is to affirm each other's strengths, not to dwell on each other's faults and weaknesses.

(5) The spiritual dimension in our lives encourages others to come to the source of true strength which is real humility before Christ.

(6) Jesus Christ is truly human because he is also truly God.

(7) The Holy Spirit is the enabling presence of God, actively involved in real life, here and now.

(8) We are the People of God and we must serve him in the world.

(9) The Scriptures are true, because he teaches us in faith more and more what the Word of God says and what it means.

(10) Worship is celebration because God is worth-ing, and he shares with us his ultimate victory over sin, evil and death.

THE LIVING FAITH

Faith is not contained and domesticated in the past. It is not fully expressed in the fleeting, elusive moments of the present. Faith is fully realized in the future as we trust him with our very lives.

So what is in the future? We can't know what, when, or how, but we do know with whom. We do know where. With him.

The Christian, then, is called to live between the "no longer" and the "not yet." Living between the times is the Biblical message. We cannot live between the times alone. We live with God and with the people of God. So who are we? We worship to search for an answer in the process of faith. So what are we to do? We serve in the world as faithful servants. So how are we to live? We are to live by faith, hope, and love. The church is the loving and

serving community of faith whose life is being renewed
each day by worship and by service.

For Further Reading:

Edge, Findley B., *The Greening of the Church,* Waco:
    Word, 1971.
Gibbs, Mark & Morton, T. Ralph, *God's Frozen People,*
    Philadelphia: Westminster, 1965; *God's Chosen People,*
    1971.
Gremillion, Joseph B., *The Gospel of Peace and Justice,*
    Roman Catholic Social Teaching Since Vatican Council
    II, Maryknoll, New York: Orbis Press, 1976.
Jaworski, Leon, *The Right and the Power,* The Prosecution
    of Watergate, New York: Reader's Digest Press, 1976.
Kraemer, Hendrick, *A Theology of the Laity,* Philadelphia:
    Westminster, 1958.
Littell, Franklin H., *The German Phoenix,* How the Ger-
    man Churches Resistance to Hitler gave birth to the
    massive lay movements to the Kirchentag and the Acad-
    emies, Garden City, New York: Doubleday and Com-
    pany, Inc., 1960.
Mouw, Richard J., *Political Evangelism,* Grand Rapids,
    Michigan: Eerdmans, 1973; *Politics and the Biblical
    Drama,* 1976.
Niebuhr, H. Richard, *Christ and Culture,* New York:
    Harper, 1951; *The Responsible Self,* 1963.
Niebuhr, Rienhold, *The Children of Light and the Children
    of Darkness,* New York: Charles Scribner's Sons, 1944;
    Moral Man and Immoral Society, 1932.
Skinner, Thomas, *If Christ Is the Answer, What Are the
    Questions?,* Grand Rapids, Michigan: Zondervan, 1974.
Wedel, Cynthia C., *Faith of Fear and Future Shock,* New
    York: Friendship Press, 1974.

The Study Guide

The major appeal of *The New Laity* is to take seriously what it means to be a Christian in such a world as ours. Specifically, this appeal is to encourage "All the people of God" to renew their personal commitment to Jesus Christ as Lord and Savior in faith and true devotion. Flowing from this renewed commitment, the challenge to grow in grace toward a more vital maturity in the spirit and the whole of the Christian life is clearly explicit. It is toward such a personal growth and the conscious development of the necessary skills for more effective service in the corporate structures of the world that this study guide is expressly written.

These six specific suggestions are made for the purpose of clarifying both the task and the methods:

1. To clarify assumptions: One good way to begin a discussion is to examine the assumptions each participant brings to the group.
2. To state common purposes: Ask each participant to write down one specific purpose and then share it with the group. To agree on a set of common purposes is to make real progress.
3. To focus expectations: Purposes and expectations are quite similar, but are not the same. Writing down expectations will help.
4. To set standards: Decisions like time, place, setting, and leadership made openly will help start the group on a constructive note.
5. To make a specific contract about methods and ground rules: Things like reading the essays under consideration in advance and agreement on the role of the leader will increase interest and participation.
6. To establish a way to evaluate results: How do you know when your purposes have been met and your expectations have been realized? The reoccurring questions throughout this study guide are:
   a. What do you think?
   b. How do you feel?
   c. What do you want to do about it?

When these questions are answered to the satisfaction of the group, the evaluation could very well be accomplished.

1. THE LAITY IN BIBLICAL PERSPECTIVE
Thomas W. Gillespie

By deliberate choice this book begins with an essay directly related to the Biblical foundation on which the rest of the essays
herein are built. The reasons are: (1) The Bible is the Word of
God, providentially inspired and provided for mankind as the
source book of both the Jewish and the Christian faith. (2) A
solid, well-thought-out and defensive Biblical position is a necessary
condition for any viable understanding for the church, for the
church's mission and purpose, and for the quality of life of the
"people of God." (3) The Biblical mandate and imperative is also
a necessary condition for any serious thrust into the world which
has the slightest hope of influencing the individual and corporate
affairs of mankind.

Dr. Gillespie has done all of us a real service by carefully building such a Biblical foundation. The word study of the term, laity,
requires a thoughtful examination. Not only the roots in Greek
and Latin, but the common use of the word, laity, and its cognate
forms illuminate our understanding of both the function and the
identity of the "people of God."

Compare and contrast the words clergy, priesthood, and laity.
Do you think Dr. Gillespie has distinguished them clearly? By
using a rather extensive examination of 1 Peter 2, does he make
his point *to you* that temple, priesthood, and sacrifices are essentially ways of expressing the redemptive ministry of Jesus and that
all the "people of God" share in the extension of that ministry?
Do you think the rather elaborate explanation of priesthood as contained in the letter to the Hebrews is clear and accurate? What does
the priesthood of all believers mean to you?

Does Dr. Gillespie present a convincing case to you? Remember
that the trick is to read it, study it, find out what you think it says
and to interpret it in your own terms, in your own lives, and for
your own reasons.

Some practical suggestions:

1. After having read this essay, can you remember the principal
   thrust of the argument? Write down *what you think* the progression of thought is.
2. After having thought about its major thesis, what difference
   does it make in your practical feelings? Write down *how you
   feel* about the Bible in general and how you feel as part of
   the people of God.
3. After having *thought* about it, and discovered for yourself
   how you *feel* about it, what do you intend to do as a result
   of your new awareness? Write down what you intend *to do*

about your being specially included in the royal priesthood, holy nation, God's own people.

General, grand ideas are fine, but specific, direct, and personal goals are better. Aren't they?

2. WORLD-WIDE VISION OF CHURCH AND WORLD
Cynthia C. Wedel

Have you ever made this vital connection between John 3:16 and 17?

God so *loved* the world

a. that he sent his Son—Whosoever believes (essential personal thrust)
b. God sent his Son into the world not to *condemn* the world but that the world might be *saved* (essential corporate thrust).

Let these two verses live in your soul and mind a while. Let them bear their own fruit in specific relationship to you. Ask the Lord who inspired their writing to encourage your reading of them. What do they mean to *you*?

Is Christ's mission through the church and the people of God to save the world? In your opinion, is this the theme of Dr. Wedel's essay?

Dr. Wedel suggests at least three major theological affirmations, all three convictions about who God is and what God is doing. (1) God is active in the world (2) God is not merely a bigger, grander, more intelligent human, but rather of a different quality. How does her conviction compare with Karl Barth's famous dictim, "You cannot say God by shouting man in a loud voice"? (3) God is good, loving, and caring.

This is an attempt to establish a foundation on which to build a vital relation between God and mankind, and between God and the world. In your opinion, is it sound Biblically? Is it right based on Christian experience? Is it good judged from practical evidence?

One of Dr. Wedel's answers to the question, "What is God doing in his world now?" is that God is forming his people together. The church's first missionaries were Peter, Paul, and Barnabas. The church has been sending missionaries abroad for over 100 years in the modern era. Why is it in your opinion that the modern ecumenical movement began in 1910 in Edinburgh, Scotland, flowing out of the missionary's concern for the whole world?

By logical extension, Vatican Council II (1961–65) has added a new dimension to the entire Christian scene. Serious consideration will be given this "new breeze of the Spirit" in Monsignor Gremillion's essay. It is mentioned here to add a distinctive flavor and to supply another illustration to the ecumenical reality.

Suggestions—write down your opinions, O.K.?

1. What do you *think* about Dr. Wedel's essay? Agree? Disagree? Don't care?
2. What do you *feel* about an international, ecumenical "people of God"?
3. What are you personally going to do about it?

"We modern Christians need more than anything else to work toward a deeper understanding of the God in whom we say we believe." The great question is: Will we see his hand in the events of our time?

Are these two sentences the key to the theme of this essay? If not, what are the key sentences in your opinion? If so, then do her examples of sciences, technology, human relations, rapid transportation, instant communications, rise in the third world (Europe and North America are first world, Russia and China are second world, Africa, Asia and Central and South America are third world) suggest a strategy to you?

What criteria would you use to judge where in the events of our times God's hand is active and at least partially visible? The moral principles of dignity of persons (intrinsic worth of people), movement toward more human concern, vital link between opportunity and responsibility may be some standards. However, Dr. Wedel leaves this an open question. What do you perceive God is doing?

3. . . . INTO THE WORLD, SO SEND I YOU
Findley B. Edge

After World War II the great push and resurgence was the church as "the people of God," both lay and clergy. It was "an idea whose time had come."

Why did it not "take off and fly"? What happened? Was it drowned in an ocean of words? Are words, even good ones, an adequate substitute for actions, deeds, implementation? Obviously Dr. Edge says no.

In this essay, the word minister means servant, as it almost always means in the New Testament. So, after trying to understand, searching for a motive like "The gospel is the power of God to everyone who believes" (Rom. 1:16), the question still is the ancient yet profoundly urgent one, "How can I be a minister where I am?"

Dr. Edge gives three kinds of suggestions:

1. *Ministry through one's vocation*—through the structures of society. He lists examples from business, advertising, multi-national corporations, and politics. Do you like these examples in the sense that you identify with them as real, as truly difficult, and as helpful to you? Can you make a list of your own examples, using his as a model of representative categories? Will you make such a list?

2. *Ministry to individuals.* Individuals and corporate structures are two distinctly different categories, yet they are so inter-meshed and interdependent that they seem to flow together.

   Motel chaplains, chapels in office buildings, caring about people's needs and immediate problems are all good, but there is more to it than a "bandaid" here and there. Do you agree or disagree that being kind and sensitive to other's feelings is a good start, but hardly a finish? Challenge yourself to come up with some of your own helpful initiatives, in specific terms, about specific people with whom you work.

3. *Support system for ministry.* Dr. Edge suggests two really important types of support—educational and group. What do you know and want to learn? How can a group, church, business, friends, really help you by encouragement, confirmation, and extended relationship over a long enough time to be truly effective?

   How can you help other people in an encouraging, supportive and effective manner?

VOCATION OF THE LAITY FROM ROMAN CATHOLIC PERSPECTIVE

4. TOWARD A FAITH OF OUR OWN
Joseph Cunneen

One of the unusual features of this book is that a wide range of Christian opinion is deliberately included as a symbol of the "new direction" toward which the new laity is pointing.

The book itself is intended *to be* a symbol of future consideration, cooperation, and productive, liberating, actual work among Christian laity. This is a beginning to explain, to explore, and to probe the essential unity in Christ which the laity already knows, feels, and does in actual experience in the world. In this sense, the laity are already the leaders of the Christian impact on the world, in the world, and for the world.

Let me point out in outline several points Joe Cunneen develops for your consideration in studying this fine essay.

As a Protestant, does it strike you as remarkable that Cunneen would develop a "common priesthood of the faithful" which is similar to the sixteenth century Protestant Reformation concept of the "priesthood of all believers"? As a Catholic, does it strike you as a common ground on which to build a brotherhood and sisterhood for all Christian laity? Ordained priests and pastors are *not* the church. Rather the church is all the "people of God" whenever, wherever, and whomever the sovereign Lord calls into his service. By the grace of God, priests and pastors are included in the people of God.

With real skill Cunneen also weaves into the fabric of the essay competence as a mark of discipleship. Pious answers and attitudes do not guarantee a suit that fits, even if the tailor goes to mass. I want a competent pilot flying the plane I am in, then I'll be happy to discuss philosophy, religion, and politics *after* we are on the ground. Work is a part of vocation, and as a Christian, competence is a distinctive mark of Christian vocation. "Work for the glory of God" has a familiar ring to it, doesn't it?

Power is a reality. Carefully read again what Cunneen says about who has it, who does not have it, and how power is used, or abused.

Specific suggestions:

1. Write down the issues which appeal to you most and which deserve special thought and discussion. General poor quality of knowledge, priesthood of all believers, competence, and power are some of mine. What are yours?

2. If you are a Protestant, look up your local Catholic priest, give him a copy of this book, and inquire about forming a group to study this book together. You could do the same with a Catholic layperson or a nun.

3. If you are a Catholic, do the same. Try to get a conversation going which includes as wide a variety of Christians as possible. In a sense, if it is local, it is real.

VOCATION OF THE LAITY FROM A WOMAN'S PERSPECTIVE

5. VOCATION FOR WOMEN TODAY
Sally Cunneen

We do not want a "Mickey Mouse" book, which reflects a false spectrum of peace and light only. Recognizing the danger of an overcritical, negative tone on the one hand, and a "sweet" generality on the other, Ms. Cunneen's essay is an example of dealing with several substantial problems, while at the same time reaffirming the basic faith in terms of real life.

The reason for including an essay written by an able Christian laywoman is to bear witness to a relatively new issue within the Christian community. The importance of the "new" identity of Christian women is massive and requires our earnest attention. Since more than 50 percent of the people of God are women, and since the cultural advance in the last few years has demanded a "zero based" approach (that is, to begin from scratch, rather than building on the old, tired, and, in my opinion, false basis), the urgent necessity is to rethink and rework the entire problem of sexuality. Attention is called to both the religious aspect of the sexuality problem and the cultural factors which in my opinion are inseparably interlaced together.

Let me list five distinctive issues which Ms. Cunneen raises with the suggestion that you work on these five and any others you think flow from them.

1. The author shares with us part of her personal pilgrimage. You have one, too, so write it down so that you can see as objectively as possible where you have been and where you want to go.

2. "Just for the record, I don't want to be a priest, but I want to make that choice myself and not have it made for me." So Ms. Cunneen rather forcefully states the obvious, namely, a choice as possible, not having been made for her by others. The logic is the same here for other professions such as doctors, lawyers, telephone repair crews, or West Point cadets.

3. The role of authority in personal decisions is a debated issue in the Roman Catholic Church, especially on birth control and related matters.

Other issues in Protestant circles are equally controversial, usually filled with more emotion than rational judgment, more heat than light. To be afraid of controversy as such is to deny our own freedom in the Lord. To love controversy and to enjoy finding our meaning in life in constant conflict is to deny the peace of God which passes all understanding.

4. "Love the Lord thy God . . . . and your neighbor as *yourself*." So the author's friend says, "Build up their egos!"

We all need victories and strokes and the confirmation of our persons. Appealing to the good in us is far better than pointing out the bad and guilty, isn't it? "You can draw more flies with honey than you can with vinegar." Right?

Compliment a friend! Say a good word for your boss or fellow worker. Smile!

5. "This basic identity does not deny female sexuality, but it refuses to be defined totally by it. While the person is thus called to wholeness . . . . ."

The whole person is the Biblical and theological summary of the human nature with which God has endowed us. Right?
So again:

1. What do you think?
2. What do you feel?
3. What are you going to do about it?

6. THE CORPORATE CALLING OF THE LAITY
Richard J. Mouw

Our assignment to Dr. Mouw was to write an essay which presented a case for both essential elements of the gospel—the personal and the corporate. The editor thinks the assignment has been carried out extremely well. However, it is up to you, the reader, to judge for yourself the effectiveness of Dr. Mouw's presentation.

Richard Mouw is a professional philosopher, a professor at Calvin College in Grand Rapids, Michigan, and a most sincere and involved Christian layman in the evangelical conservative tradition of the Christian Reformed Church. His two books, *Political Evangelism* and *Politics and the Biblical Drama* (Eerdmans; Grand Rapids, 1973–1976) are well worth reading and carefully studying.

Dr. Mouw uses the insurance agent as his central example. What is your struggle as you try to be a Christian businessman, salesman, plumber, or whatever? Write down some of your own tensions and frustrations as you try to match the demands of the gospel with the hard-nosed pressure of the world.

Do you agree with Dr. Mouw that the gospel is complex, a many-sided splendor? What is your opinion of the three levels he mentions: (1) creation; (2) sin; (3) redemption? Do each of these apply to both the personal and the corporate? In your own life in what ways do these elements conflict, or complement each other?

What you do think of his three suggestions: (1) consciousness raising; (2) real study; (3) decision—using your good judgment? Frankly, I like his idea that we *do not* need a new gospel.

The old gospel which has been proclaimed in sermon and song through the years has all the necessary elements in it. For example, the so-called conservative Christians have been singing, "Joy to the world, the Lord is come, let earth receive her King." The *political* implications of the gospel are already there. The *economic* aspects of the gospel are apparent when George Beverly Shea sings, "I'd rather have Jesus than silver or gold." The *racial* relations are clear when we teach our children to sing, "Red and yellow, black and white, they are precious in his sight." What all of us need to hear again is that the "old, old story of Jesus and his love" is true and more than enough to transform our own lives and the lives of the whole world. We already believe it. Dr. Mouw is effective in reminding us that "each time we hear it the more wonderful it seems."

(2) *Real Study*—Threatening? Frightening? Perhaps! But you really don't expect magic, do you? You are willing to work hard at your profession, to keep up or at least try to. "Work hard" is a sign of honor. Why is the demand so different in religion? Read what Dr. Mouw says again. Convinced? Seek out someone nearby and ask to study with them, talk to them, listen to them. Disciplined thought is hard work. Let there be no illusions. Pay the price. Athletes do; musicians do. Why not lay theologians?

(3) *Decide what to do.* Mouw uses the word, *casuistry.* Perhaps it is a new word for you. According to the *Dictionary of Christian Ethics,* edited by John Macquarrie (Philadelphia: Westminster Press, 1967, p. 47): "In its widest sense, casuistry is the art of deciding what is right or wrong in particular cases where general norms (standards) are not precise enough." Decision making is a problem of its own. When you add moral or right to the process, it becomes a double problem.

Do you appreciate what Mouw is trying to say in conclusion about "the nature of our mandate"?

"A chosen race, a royal priesthood, a holy nation, God's own people" (1 Peter 2:9). Honor all men. Love the brotherhood. Fear God (1 Peter 2:17). What does this mean to you?

Do you agree that as a part of the definition of the gospel itself is the command to go into all the world and proclaim the gospel—physically, professionally, and in all other spheres of human activity?

What do you think?

How do you feel?

What do you intend to do about it in your unique circumstances?

7. ROMAN CATHOLIC SOCIAL TEACHING
Monsignor Joseph B. Gremillion

In the words of Monsignor Gremillion such an open cooperation and the new willingness to listen to each other would have been "unthinkable" a short twenty years ago.

Perhaps one reason why it is so hard to appreciate the massive impact of Vatican Council II on the Roman Catholic Church and on the entire world is that it is so relatively recent. Catholics themselves find it strange and somewhat threatening to realize even in a partial manner the revolutionary implications of such a "refreshing new breeze from the Holy Spirit." There are still literally millions of Protestants who have not yet even begun to think about the practical effects of Vatican Council II.

We are privileged to have this introductory essay into recent Roman Catholic social thought written by one of the real authorities in such matters. Monsignor Gremillion has not only played a leading role in putting at least some of the implications into practice, but he has also written the comprehensive book which makes available the actual documents in one place (*The Gospel of Peace and Justice,* Maryknoll, New York: Orbis Press, 1976).

SPECIFIC SUGGESTIONS ABOUT CONTENT

1. Read the essay carefully with special reference to the open invitation for all people to consider the intrinsic human dignity of each individual person.
2. Notice the seriousness with which the documents address the massive problems of corporate society.
3. Observe the three major institutions of society which are identified as cooperating for the common good, rather than competing (productive property, human work and participation, and the governmental structures).
4. Translate these three institutions as private industry, human relations, and governmental participation.
5. Think about the necessity of each of these elements working together for the public interest.

SPECIFIC QUESTIONS ABOUT RELIGIOUS CONCERNS

1. Do the Biblical passages in the beginning of the essay carry with them an urgent appeal as far as you personally are concerned?
2. Does the assertion from *Christianity and Social Progress* (1961) that the major purpose of the Church is that all who enter "may find salvation as well as the fullness of a more excellent life" appeal to you?
3. What is the relationship between personal faith and corporate responsibility?
4. Is it proper in your opinion to extend the concept of "neighbor" to all people?
5. Do you find it encouraging for the Roman Catholic Church to be actively pursuing practical ways to improve the quality of life for people all over the world?
6. How can you be most effective in serving God where you are, with what you now have, for reasons which are urgent for you, and from motives which you consider to be most compelling?

SPECIFIC RECOMMENDATIONS FOR FURTHER STUDY

1. Get a copy of Monsignor Gremillion's book and begin to study it. What does it say? What does it mean?
2. Seek out other concerned Christians and talk about the monu-

mental advance of the Roman Catholic Church since Vatican Council II.
3. Do your part in breaking down the artificial barriers between fellow Christians, as you examine seriously any prejudice you may or may not have.
4. Become more aware of the new ways you can grow in both personal and corporate influence for the Lord.

These recommendations may seem "meek and mild," but let me assure you that there really is a new day in Christian relationships and that you can be a part of this exciting and faithful breakthrough.

8. MORAL FOUNDATIONS OF GOVERNMENT
Leon Jaworski

In my opinion, Mr. Jaworski knows with his obvious intelligence and feels with his obvious sensitivity the harsh facts of how it is. A lawyer deals with so much of the seamy side of life—especially one who played a role in the war criminal trials after World War II and in the Watergate and Koreagate affairs. Jaworski is well aware of the weaknesses, frailties, and subtle temptations of both power and greed. Against his background, it is particularly moving to me to feel uplifted and ennobled by one who also knows and feels the power and majesty of the simple words like honesty, liberty, justice, and integrity.

By quoting the text, "For he looked forward to the city which has foundations, whose builder and maker is God" (Heb. 11:10), Jaworski puts these grand words in a distinctly theological frame and applies them to both personal characteristics and corporate reality.

"The old truth remains, you see, that you cannot achieve good by evil means." I am sure Mr. Jaworski would agree that we do justify our means by our ends, for there is hardly any other viable standard by which to measure the morality of either means or ends. The hard question is where can we draw the line in our determination of what ends justify what means.

In answering this hard question, Mr. Jaworski suggests a series of principles derived both from the Judeo-Christian tradition and from the Constitution of the United States and related documents.

With a number of appropriate examples, Mr. Jaworski quotes Dr. Butler regarding the precepts of liberty and the dictates of justice. A concept is a basic framework of an idea and a precept is the content derived by experience which is poured into a conceptual framework. So after having experienced liberty, we raise it from an abstract theory to an actual precept of reality. By the same logic, justice is not an idealized virtue as discussed at length by the ancient Greeks, for example, but rather the dictates of justice here means that liberty and justice for all are practiced in the legal structures of society.

The need is to rebuild public confidence not by more eloquent phrases, but by public demonstration of the fact of liberty and justice for all. Lack of knowledge and meaning coupled with the lack of foresight are partial reasons, but lack of the will to do the right, the just, and the good lies at the root of our American dilemma. When ethical standards are irrelevant, then the disease is radical (that is, at the roots).

The principle Mr. Jaworski suggests by quoting de Tocqueville is goodness. "America is great because America is good, and if America ever ceases to be good, America will cease to be great."

The example of Thomas Jefferson adds the principle of honesty. Sir Thomas More contributes integrity. Henry L. Stimson illumines the scene with honor, trust, and faith.

"Are these just empty phrases . . . or are they still as radiant, as inspirational and as binding in our pursuits as they were to these great founders of freedom and seekers of justice?"

You, the reader, must answer this question for yourselves.

9. FROM JERUSALEM TO NASHVILLE:
URBAN MISSION FOR SOUTHERN CHRISTIANS
Donald W. Shriver

Both Leon Jaworski's and Don Shriver's contributions to this book were originally formulated as addresses which were made in speech, rather than in written form. However, each carries its own distinctive flavor, wit, and extremely significant content. Another comparison is that both addresses are examples of how to apply the ethical and moral ideals to corporate structures within our society, to government and to cities, respectively.

Ethics is a rational attempt to develop standards, derived from worthy sources, by which to judge an act or series of actions with respect to good or bad, right or wrong. Morality, on the other hand, is the practical relationship among persons which is evaluated on the basis of the standards one professes to believe and to which one has a serious commitment.

There is an acute awareness that the conflicts between how it "ought" to be and how it "is" are massive and threatening. However, both speakers make an encouraging contribution precisely at the points of the conflicts; namely, by holding our minds and hearts close to the ethical standards practically all of us say we believe.

There is a lot of Bible, theology, history, and interpretation of "issues that seem to emerge for us who live and move and have our contemporary Christian being in the cities" in Dr. Shriver's presentation. Is it clear to you what the basic issues are? Do the ideals we profess conflict with the perceived realities in your private world? Do you understand the enormity of the journey from Jerusalem to Nashville? If you think you do, why not write a paragraph or two about your own personal journey? If you do not, why don't you read this really magnificent address again, slowly, thoughtfully, prayerfully with a specific goal of writing your own story into it?

A. What is the word of judgment? It is a long way from eighth century, B.C., Israel, to Little Rock, Kalamazoo, Modesta, Brooklyn, or wherever. "Do justice . . . love kindness . . . walk humbly with your God" (Micah 6:8). What does that say *to you?* What does it *mean* to you?

B. Do we as humans really want to live together on this spaceship Earth? If so, how?
What *will the church do to help?*
What *should* the church do to help?
What *can* the church do to help?

C. What is word from the Lord about our public and private babels—towers, or otherwise?
How many times will the Lord have to smash our idols before we finally pick up the clue—"Thou shall have no other gods before me"?

What is the latest example of the world in your own front yard?

Shriver's three examples of what is happening in the five projects he mentions are worthy of more consideration. Can you think of others?

What is the eternal dimension of the vision of a city not made with hands *for you?*

10. STYLES IN CHRISTIAN MISSIONS
Howard C. Blake

In many ways this essay could be considered the pivotal essay of this book. Why? Because Howard and his most able wife, Peggy, were the inspiration behind the conference, the new laity concept, and the preparation of this book. Because Howard and Peggy are living examples of the winsome, appealing style which is advocated in this essay, and by the other efforts connected with this new laity understanding.

The Southern Baptist churches have a most attractive phrase, *Living Proof*, which Howard and Peggy personify. After all the good logic and careful reasoning about faith and its vital connection with life have been displayed, the age-old most persuasive argument is still the quality of a devoted life which demonstrates the supreme value of true faith.

Blake's essay is such a demonstration. The mood is aimed at the heart. The appeal is aimed at the life we actually live. The structure is aimed at action. The thrust of thought is aimed at *how*.

"How can Christian service in the world be more effective?" Is this the key question?

The movement of thought begins with the personal and progresses toward the corporate. Perhaps this is one of the most difficult transitions of which we humans are capable. Many faithful servants of God have been "hung up" on this shift. The traditional model has been for the churches to inspire and train an individual and to send him/her forth into the world to influence the corporate structures and systems.

Blake is suggesting that this is necessary, because without a reliable moral person no society can long exist. However, it is not sufficient, because the corporate structures are more than the individuals who lead them or who are led by them.

The personal moral pattern of thought and action is not adequate for the massive task of changing the unjust systems of social organization.

So this author and you and I are reaching for practical ways for the faithful person to influence more effectively the institutions of society for good and for Christ.

THE ADVERSARY STANCE

Is this new approach appealing to you? If you are a leader in industry or government, can you develop an effective way to let your faith show? We need help from those already in power who are Christians. Can you see yourself as brave enough to try?

A NEW WIND

Surely the old, wornout, false division of the "two party system" in all the churches is seen as both superficial and destructive. Are *both* personal integrity *and* social passion for justice combined in your head and in your heart? I think it is for Howard Blake. I feel it *can* be in you!

A FRESH ATTACK

Surely Vatican Council II has opened up vast new areas of practical cooperation and mutual encouragement to the whole of the Christian witness in the world. Not that the problems are solved nor the many questions answered, but is not a basis of mutual trust (worthy of our best) being provided by the Lord himself?

Can we see together that in the world persons of good will from all the churches are already working together in productive work? Why not concentrate on raising the level of ethical standards and moral behavior? Why? For practical and religious reasons!

Basically, you already know what is right in terms of being honest, fair, responsible, and moral. So why not seek to understand how to be more aware and more effective in the corporate structures in which we all live and on which we so desperately depend?

21 CHARACTERISTICS

Read over Blake's list of specific suggestions again. Write your opinions on each of them. Rediscover for yourself how deep your personal motivations are as you determine how serious you are in being the kind of person who can help. Rediscover for yourself how you can be more effective in virtues and in service to your Lord.

Please take the gospel personally. Please take your own life seriously. Please take the Lord faithfully and let him show you a better way.

11. WORSHIP AND SERVICE
A. Fred Swearingen

"The purpose of this essay is to reach for a more vital connection between worship and service."

Do you see the superior importance of a fresh awareness of self-identity inseparably linked with a transforming relationship with Almighty God?

"Who am I?" Is this your question which seeks a vital answer for you in worship? "What am I to do?" Is this your question which seeks a vital answer for you in service?

The theme of this essay is echoed in the assertion that we ask both questions at the same time.

Is this vital connection clear to you? Do you really believe it?

SEEING BEYOND THE STAINED GLASS WINDOWS

What do you think of this progression of thought? How do you feel about the movement from church to world? What can you personally do to make such a transition in your own life?

FROM WORSHIP TO ETHICS

oes what we say we believe practically affect what we actu
rite down a list of particulars.

*Yes*_____ *No*_____

THE WORD/DEED TENSION

Is real worship merely words to you? List the ways you can turn mere words into real deed.

Worship is event

_____ _____

1   10
Evaluate your experience

THE BEST IS YET TO BE

The core of true faith points to the future.
Right?   Wrong?
How do you perceive true faith?

GRASSHOPPERS?

Does the church have a "grasshopper neurosis"?
*Yes*_____ *No*_____
Can courage be generated by faith?
For you?
*Yes*_____ *No*_____
How?
*Yes*_____ *No*_____
What is ahead for us?
For you, personally?
For our world, corporately?

A VISION?

Swearingen lists ten affirmative statements. After having reread them, make a list of your own. Give reasons *why,* on what grounds, from what motives.

THE LIVING FAITH

Write down several reasons why you think this book ends with worship and service. What do you think? How do you feel? What are you willing to do?